PATHWAYS FOR COMMUNICATION

PATHWAYS FOR COMMUNICATION

Books and Libraries in
the Information Age

D J FOSKETT

CLIVE BINGLEY  LONDON

Copyright © D J Foskett 1984
First published 1984 by Clive Bingley Limited, The Library Association, 7 Ridgmount Street, London WC1E 7AE and printed in England by Redwood Burn Limited, Trowbridge, Wilts.

All rights reserved. No part of this publication may be photocopied, recorded or otherwise reproduced, stored in a retrieval system or transmitted in any form or by any electronic or mechanical means without the prior permission of the copyright holder and publisher.

British Library Cataloguing in Publication Data

Foskett, D. J.
    Pathways for communication.
    1. Libraries and society
    I. Title
    021   Z716.4

ISBN 0-85157-356-8

Typeset by Allset in 12 on 13 point Aldine Roman

1234587868584

CONTENTS

1	Information and understanding	1
2	Communication and chronicles	12
3	Communication and society	21
4	Information and the psychology of users	35
5	Keepers and finders	47
6	Technology and culture	60
7	Theory and practice	75
8	Memory and anticipation	88
9	Looking for answers	101
10	A reading society	116
	References	129
	Index	135

Man is the helper and interpreter of Nature. He can only act and understand in so far as he has observed Nature's order practically or theoretically. Outside this he has no knowledge or power.

Francis Bacon *Novum Organum* Aphorism 1

Chapter 1

INFORMATION AND UNDERSTANDING

Among the many requisites for the survival of humanity in an age of nuclear power, which may bring in its train an age of leisure, whether chosen or involuntary, access to information is by no means the least. When the deschooler Ivan Illich wrote that 'at its best the library is the prototype of a convivial tool', he celebrated the fact that, at its best, the library responds to the needs of individual people by giving them free access to learning resources, which they can select for themselves.

On this view, the computer seems to offer just the opportunity that the individual would wish to have. By designating 1982 as 'Information Technology Year', the British Government recognized that what had come to be known as 'the new technology' ought to be harnessed to meet Society's requirements in the communication of information. Following on the campaign within the United Nations for a New International Economic Order, Unesco, stimulated by pressure from countries of the Third World, proposed the forming of a New World Information and Communication Order. And the General Assembly of the UN, at the end of 1981, recognizing 'the fundamental importance of communications infrastructures as an essential element in the economic and social development of all countries', proclaimed 1983 as World Communications Year, for the development of communications infrastructures.

In all these activities, as in widespread, vague and earnest arguments about the 'Information Age', it is as if we all knew what we mean by the word 'Information', and Society, through its co-operative institutions, has both the skill and the will to organize the appropriate supplies. Yet the substance of the actual discussions shows that neither of these two assumptions stands up to inspection. We have a situation which would satisfy Humpty Dumpty's philological criterion; each group involved with what the Oxford English Dictionary calls 'training, instruction . . . intelligence, news' uses the word 'information' to suit its own specialist purposes, and devises 'infrastructures' accordingly.

The most powerful of these groups — those engaged in the news media and in the telecommunications industry — look at the question of infrastructures almost entirely from the point of view of the producers and transmitters of factual data. When these relate to current events the 'information' conveyed by radio and television has the attractive quality of seeming almost instantaneous: the 'man on the spot' tells us what is happening at the time. The impact is immediate and often dramatic, but the instant information usually precedes equally instant oblivion, because more events occur, which must be transmitted equally swiftly. Since the impact of disaster exceeds the impact of happiness, the 'News' tends to record a dismal succession of catastrophes, and the receiver of such news appreciates it all the more in that it concerns someone else.

Information in the guise of factual data also relates to another area of human activity, one in which a far less powerful group engages — those in libraries and centres of documentation. For many years, some of these practitioners have made strenuous efforts to improve their power status by detaching themselves from their materials, their library base, and adopting the style of 'information officers'. Theoretical advances in the discipline have become 'information science'. While we may applaud these efforts, and understand the motives which lie behind them, the harsh fact remains that they have met with little success outside the profession which they seek to elevate. Even in industry, where the most important advances have occurred, information services suffered heavily when recession struck and economies were enforced.

This seems most strange when we are supposedly in the information age, and I believe that one of the many factors at the heart of the matter lies in this failure to arrive at any agreement over what we mean when we talk about information. How is it, for example, that the General Information Programme of Unesco will have nothing to do with the International Programme for the Development of Communication? Their documents speak a similar language but mean quite different things, especially when dealing with infrastructures and meeting people's needs. Even the meaning of 'need' in this context has not been sufficiently explored.

The IPDC undoubtedly attracts the attention of those in high government levels, while the GIP does not, despite the success of the GIP and its predecessors at Unesco in developing the world science information system known as UNISIST. This illustrates one aspect of the problem. As John Ziman puts it, Science is Public Knowledge: scientific data have a kind of neutrality which is thought to be free from political or any other subjective colouring. Not everyone accepts this: Barry Barnes makes a convincing case, in his analysis of T S Kuhn's theory of scientific revolutions, for the view that paradigms reflect goals and interests that are socially determined. But generally speaking, the data of the physical and natural sciences are accepted the world over. Tables of constants do not as a rule provoke polemics, and it is not the simple equation $E = Mc^2$ which inspires political controversy. There is enough evidence to show that it is true for Hiroshima as well as for Alamogordo. The social behaviour arising from our understanding of the equation causes the problems.

Different understandings or interpretations of the word 'information' have a similar result. Everyone seems to agree on the benefits of quick and accurate dissemination of information, and on our bounden duty to organize the necessary infrastructure. Only when we maintain that our own understanding, our own definition, is the correct one do we fall into the Universal Context Fallacy and ignore all evidence to the contrary.

What, then, should we mean by Information, and who needs it? These questions cannot be answered satisfactorily if we continue to regard Information as a parcel of factual data which requires simply to be packaged and moved from here to there. We do not go to the play of *Hamlet* for Information on the history of Denmark, but only the most abandoned Philistine would deny that *Hamlet* has human value. It has been said that half the entire work force in the United States is engaged in the Information industry; does this include university professors of English? And is this Information industry an end in itself?

We shall find no sensible answers, that is, answers which make sense to us in human terms, unless and until we recognize that Information may have precise meanings related to precise contexts, but only in a very general way can we describe it so that the practitioners in these various contexts will acknowledge their common interests. These relate, beyond question, to our way of life and to the sort of society we hope to live in. Those who produce what they call Information, in their various contexts, rely on having consumers, those who wish to receive this Information. One group of producers, the newspaper editors, journalists, radio and television producers, give the group of consumers, what they think it ought to have, claiming to use the market as the index of need. The positive act resides with the producers. Librarians, traditionally, collect and look after the records of information in their care, giving the consumers what they ask for. The positive act resides with the consumers.

Generally speaking, then, Information consists of statements made by individuals about concepts which they have assimilated into their store of knowledge — a structure of concepts already assimilated. Information service consists in the use of such statements for the benefit of others. Primary producers include journalists and broadcasters who observe events and relay their observations through the news media; writers and commentators who add their own interpretations of such events; scientists who cause events to happen in their laboratories and relay their observations through specialist books and journals; imaginative writers who illuminate events by the power of their imagination. Secondary producers include editors, publishers, booksellers and librarians; all who provide or facilitate access to the various sources. The lack of communication between these groups becomes all the more reprehensible when we see that they have a great deal in common. They are all concerned with the transmission of concepts from one mind to another; and they all belong to a social organization in order to bring this transmission to success. Only by establishing and participating in such an organization can these individuals achieve the aims for the sake of which they involve themselves with Information. The aims derive from the view that a certain collection of concepts held in the mind of one individual will have value for others and so should be entered into the social organization for passing them on.

We now have an imposing array of producers, and most of the time they do not just enter their information into the system as bald statements of fact. They expect to have a group of consumers for whom their information has a particular value, and they tailor its presentation accordingly. The mechanism of transmission also has an effect: the same statements will look very different in the pages of *Nature* and on the television screen. This underlines the motivation which lies behind the will to communicate — the producer believes that certain information in his possession will have value for others. His view of the nature of the consumers will influence the way in which he describes his information. However much he may claim that his statements are true, that they have an objective value, nevertheless the producer hopes that the consumers of his information will take the same view of it as himself. He hopes not only to inform, but to persuade. The sharing of information will lead to the sharing of a point of view.

A point of view represents the association of a number of concepts organized on the basis of personal experience. Each of us has a unique personality because the life experience of each is unique — no two people live exactly similar lives. The organization of common experience constitutes society, and it is from this source that information derives its value. Through our experience we associate concepts and ideas of the world around us, and when we perceive that certain associations please us or enable us to cope better with the world, we are often impelled to pass them on, to communicate them to someone else. We consider that our knowledge of the world may be socially useful. The stock of such socially available concepts forms the foundation of the society we build for ourselves. A structure of society develops out of the ever-increasing stock of socially available concepts which have common acceptance. The stock itself becomes available through the media and pathways for communication.

Libraries are the organizations which society establishes for collecting the stock, and librarians are one of the groups who have the responsibility for making it available. This makes it all the more important that librarians should understand how they fit into the communication process, and their relationship to others involved in the process should be clear to all of them. Only when this happens shall we succeed in dispelling the mists and confusions which surround the use of the word 'Information'.

For Information itself is a social concept. It arises from the notion of sharing knowledge for the benefit of others, and it cumulates from the results of action and behaviour stimulated by such sharing. Our own knowledge of the world may be private and personal, precisely because it comes from our own experience. We cannot *know* someone else's *knowledge*, because knowledge itself is information — the publicly available stock — which has been received, sorted and assimilated into a human mind. By 'publicly available', I of course mean to include information we gain from our own perceptions of nature and the physical world we live in. Percepts are transformed into concepts when they are successfully assimilated into a structure of ideas already assembled in the mind, and which they help to enlarge and enhance. Each mind is unique, and to that extent each of us is an original. Information, therefore, is that element of our knowledge which is publicly available and which we can all share and pass around to each other. If we have great imaginative powers, we can perceive 'in a flash' how concepts can relate to other concepts in ways previously unthought of, and so create new forms and new insights which have universal value. When Wordsworth wrote of Peter Bell

    a primrose by the river's brim,
    a simple primrose was to him,
    and it was nothing more

he meant that Peter Bell lacked the imaginative quality necessary to transform the concept of 'primrose', as Wordsworth himself could transform it, into a life-enhancing experience with significant value for others. A great writer communicates such insights and saves the rest of us the trouble of building up the same experience by the laborious process of consciously assembling all the necessary bits of information. And although common opinion often expresses the contrary, scientists and artists all contribute both to the building blocks and flashes of insight.

    At the Royal Academy banquet in 1887, T H Huxley put it like this: 'I imagine that it is the business of the artist and of the man of letters to reproduce and fix forms of the imagination, to which the mind will afterwards recur with pleasure; so, based upon the same great principle by the same instinct, if I may so call it, it is the business of the man of science to symbolize and fix, and represent to our mind in some easily recallable shape, the order, and the symmetry, and the beauty that prevail throughout Nature ...'.

Over specialization, leading to artificial barriers to understanding between scientist and men of letters, and even between different groups of scientists, he considered one of the greatest obstacles to progress in every field. Today, this over-specialization causes a narrowness of vision which tends to focus the mind on details — bits of information — to the neglect of the structure as a whole.

Yet it is precisely the overall structure which gives us our general picture of the world and leads to greater understanding of how to cope. The more we succeed in integrating new information into what we know already, the greater our understanding. We may not agree with the author of the book of Ecclesiasticus that 'the wisdom of a learned man cometh by opportunity of leisure', but the search for wisdom offers the only hope for survival in the age of the nuclear deterrent. Knowledge tempered and refined through human experience, the enhancement of the individual self, what Bronowski has called the identity of Man, leads to wisdom, the ability to understand how new experience fits into old, and why it is that different people have different points of view. Wisdom enables us to make a rational interpretation of experience, both our own and that of the common stock of society. It is a two-way process: we construct our view of reality through social experience, and we add our conclusions and opinions to the common stock in the hope of sharing them with others. If I labour the point, it is because I believe that there is now a desperate need for this kind of wisdom, the communication of such rational interpretations in order to promote understanding between people. The eminent American librarian who once said, in my hearing, that he believed that the American form of librarianship was the best in the world, and that all other countries should imitate it, had obviously never thought that the social experience of other countries might differ fundamentally from the American. Even the supposedly 'neutral science' has to be accepted with caution, as Robin Horton has shown in his analysis of the point of view of West Africans. What we look upon as primitive societies make slow progress in their economic and social development because they lack a communications infrastructure. They suffer not only from unreliable electricity supplies, but also from inadequate records. They have social memories, to be sure, but oral transmission cannot equal the stock of information available in libraries and communicated through advanced technology. They lack good weather forecasts because they have no satellite pictures to show what the next winds may bring, even though the experienced elders — the wise men of the tribe — may make good guesses. They have little technology even for basic needs, and starvation haunts them while vast stores of foodstuffs moulder away in Europe and the United States. Yet, as Horton shows, such communities certainly have the mental power to form structures of concepts; they are perfectly able to organize their thoughts through language and speech.

Horton compares this slow rate of development, in a world of space travel, to the game of Grandmother's Footsteps: each generation can achieve small adjustments in the system of social beliefs, but remains unaware of innovation because it has no way of referring back to the ideas of former generations 'frozen' in writing, and preserved in books and libraries.

The root of the problem does not lie in ignorance of the new technology: every African university has its own computers. The biggest problem in the information age in World Communications Year, does not lie in how to produce information. On the contrary, the producers happily turn out millions of items every day. Nor does the problem lie in methods of handling information: library shelves are full of books and journals describing such methods. Their authors point with pride to that great American information industry, and whole forests are destroyed in order to proclaim the advent of the paperless society. The industry owes its success to the efficiency with which modern technology can transfer bits of information from here to there. The producers are happy that the flow keeps going, and it does not matter that libraries may devotedly acquire books which no one ever reads, while newspapers, radio and television keep up a constant supply of information which no one ever remembers, because it is trivial and of no social significance.

The technology is basic, right enough, and I do not suggest that we should attempt to do without it. As William Morris prophesied, no doubt with reluctance, that road leads to Nowhere. The Mexico City Declaration on Cultural Policies, from the Unesco World Conference in 1982 recognizes that: 'The world has undergone profound changes in recent years. The progress of science and technology has changed man's place in the world and the nature of his social relations... Every culture represents a unique and irreplaceable body of values since each people's traditions and forms of expression are its most effective means of demonstrating its presence in the world'.

The biggest problem in the Information Age is to ensure that the progress of science and technology does not lead to the extinction of unique and irreplaceable bodies of values. Several delegates to the World Conference expressed alarm at the tendency towards standardization and the possibility that advanced communications technology might lead to the cultural dominance of one particular pattern over all others.

An equally important conference took place just before: the World Congress on Books, also organized by Unesco. This produced the 'London Declaration: towards a reading society'. Item 2 in the Declaration says: 'Books, we believe, retain their pre-eminence as the carriers of knowledge, education and cultural values in human society. They serve both national development and the enrichment of individual human life. They foster better understanding between peoples and strengthen the desire for peace in the minds of men, to which Unesco is dedicated'.

The question to which we have to address ourselves now is how to use the advances in science and technology in order to recognize and communicate that information which promotes understanding of, and sympathy with, the cultural heritage of other people, their point of view. The mere transmission of information as an end in itself may well result in the opposite: if we are surfeited with honey, we begin to loathe the taste of sweetness, and a surfeit of unrelated bits of information will promote neither understanding nor sympathy.

Chapter 2

COMMUNICATION AND CHRONICLES

How we express ourselves most effectively when we wish to communicate our information to others has been the subject of a great deal of discussion and controversy. The echoes of the famous 'Two Cultures' battle between C P Snow and F R Leavis have by no means died away; many of the issues are dealt with by Sir Peter Medawar in his nicely named book *Pluto's Republic*. The inhabitants of this realm, who prefer rhapsodic intellection to humdrum ratiocination (practised by such as Socrates, Descartes and Kant), include practitioners of 'scientism', who apply their mistaken idea of scientific method to moral questions of Restoration comedy, and of 'poetism', who apply literary standards of valuation to scientific theories. As with all types of information, the specific criteria for judging presentation vary according to the context in which the information is presented.

Successful presentation means that real communication has taken place. The recipient of the information presented has not only heard and understood, but has also come to understand the point of view of the presenter. He may not agree with it but at least it makes sense to him. 'Real' communication is a two-way affair, and the necessary understanding actually begins with the presenter, who must first take the trouble to understand the state of mind of the recipient. If he does not do this, his presentation will probably be totally biassed towards his own point of view. Newton was famous for the clarity and simplicity of his style, but even he was not above criticism, as evidenced by the well known letter from William Molyneux to Sir Hans Sloane in 1697: 'I hear Mr Newton's Phil. Nat. Prin. Math. is out of press and that he designs a 2nd edition. Pray advise him to make it a little more plain to Readers not so well versed in abstruse Mathematicks, a few Marginal Notes and references and Quotations will doe the business'.

Communication forms the basis and the necessary element in understanding of and at least some sympathy with, the views of both the two parties. It is not merely statements of fact that occur, but our interpretation of their meaning in the general social context. This applies even when an apparently simple statement is made. If I am told that the specific heat of mercury is 70.62, and I have no interest whatever in mercury, still less in its specific heat, then that particular statement has no meaning for me. No communication has occurred. Communication occurs when someone states a view of events, of the world around us, in such a way as to evoke a positive response in the minds of others.

Much of the confusion, and indeed irritation, that has surrounded the 'two cultures' controversy and its successors, has stemmed from misleading statements about the nature of such simple statements. When C P Scott of the *Manchester guardian* made his famous pronouncement, 'Facts are sacred; comment is free', he was, in effect, taking the same point of view as many scientists who affirm the objectivity of science as the description of the natural world. Reality is out there, runs the argument, and exists independently of the human mind; any description of it therefore should aim to exclude the influence of a human personality. 'It appeared to the writer' becomes the substitute for 'I thought'. The result, as any journalist knows, is that these plain descriptions lack precisely that element most likely to secure effective communication. When dealing with facts, just as much as with ideas, which may be new and strange, the bridge across which they can travel from one mind to another must consist of what is already held in common. The most soundly based element of this is a common humanity, a common appreciation of the human value of the publicly available information. New facts, descriptions of new events, become acceptable as part of the stock only in so far as they relate to it in a way that can be understood by at least part of society. In T S Kuhn's paradigm thesis, events and observations which puzzle, and create tensions in the paradigm — the commonly accepted view — will, if they represent reality and are not simply errors, eventually result in the amendment or overturning of the old paradigm and its replacement by a new one.

Such a scientific 'revolution', like any other revolution, has to come from a sudden access of popular energy and enthusiasm. Whitehead's account of the Royal Society meeting at which the Astronomer Royal produced experimental evidence to support Einstein's prediction that rays of light are bent near the sun strikes just such a dramatic note: 'The whole atmosphere of tense interest was exactly that of the Greek drama; we were the chorus commenting on the decree of destiny as disclosed in the development of a supreme incident . . . a great adventure in thought had at length come safely to shore'.

The use of expressions like 'Greek drama' and 'chorus commenting' presupposes that they will have a greater significance than just the words themselves because they relate to a wide-ranging context of thought, far wider indeed than astronomy or Einstein's physics. In making this assumption, Whitehead had in mind the general cultural heritage of the educated European. It is unlikely that he would have used the same imagery with an audience of Chinese.

The cultural heritage, of which scientific paradigms form an important element, plays a major role in the shaping of the individual personality. Similarly, the individual scientist or artist repays his debt by making his own unique contribution to the progress of the heritage, which does not stand still, but grows and feeds upon the inspirations of its children.

The inspiration will be the greater according to the degree to which each individual achieves a harmony between the several forces which shape his personality: his own personal experience of the world, the current scientific paradigm, the collective social view and the type of society he aspires to live in. By communicating this harmony to others, an individual influences the way society develops by creating a popular enthusiasm for a particular cause, and popular energy to pursue it.

A major factor, then, in a successful act of communication must reside in the personality of the author. By stimulating those features which lie in a common humanity, the author creates an alertness, a disposition to understand, in the minds of his audience or his readers. They are ready to listen to what he has to say and to give it their serious consideration. This involves taking the trouble to assess the significance of his message, his information, and the extent to which they are prepared to assimilate it into their own existing pattern of thinking.

It must be acknowledged, in fact, that the human personality is always present in an act of communication. If this were not so, Gutenberg's soldiers of lead would indeed have not only conquered the world, but also driven out the personal lecture. The invention of printing from movable type revolutionized communication, education and learning, by making possible the mass production of cheap books, but this has not resulted in the extinction of professors. Radio and television have added yet another technology for disseminating information, and given the professors an audience undreamt of by Socrates, Descartes or Kant, but on the other hand this has not resulted in the demise of the book. The paperless society has no more relation to the world than Edison's boast in 1913 that the invention of the cinema would soon abolish the need for books.

All these advances in technology provide excellent opportunities for the improvement of communication and the advancement of learning, and I do not for one moment underrate their importance. My point, however, is that they do not, *of themselves*, provide the yeast for the bread of knowledge. Any successful lecturer knows that the human relationship between speaker and audience creates the conditions for successful communication. In the printed word, success comes to the extent that the writer's style succeeds in approaching the same relationship. The human personality is always present because this is what determines the point of view that is being communicated. The disposition to accept this point of view depends on the harmony achieved between author and audience, between producer and consumer, and this harmony depends on the information in a message — the content — and the order of ideas in its presentation — the form. The dialectical interplay between content and form makes the dynamism which gives any presentation its total impact. Exciting ideas may crowd into a writer's mind, but unless he succeeds in imposing some order into their relationship, they will remain there like peas in a bag, in Vygotsky's memorable phrase. They will not be organized into a recognizable and acceptable theme. Referring to this concept of a significant theme presented in an organized whole, Buffon added the comment that has passed into the realm of proverb: the subjects have their own existence independent of the writer, but the presentation is unique: 'Ces choses sont hors de l'homme, le style c'est l'homme même'. The successful speaker, writer, artist, no matter what the subject, allows the warmth of his own personality to colour his presentation and give it human value.

We use this human presence as the foundation of the process of communication in order to share the original experience, so that in our encounter with what the presenter makes publicly available, we reach out from our own personality to embrace his information and so enlarge our own conceptions. In the teaching of science, students carry out well-known experiments just in order to have first-hand experience, not only of how to manage laboratory equipment, but also to understand the process of reasoning from the activity of experimenting to the forming of theories and the prediction of future results. The extension of this learning technique made possible by television is admirably demonstrated by the Christmas Lectures for Children at the Royal Institution in London. Each year a famous scientist gives a series of lectures, or rather performances, in which he presents his subject with the able assistance of 'volunteers' from the audience to carry out the experiments. The audience themselves have the benefit of the physical presence of the speaker and his assistants: the television viewers have only the electronic image, but also have the compensation of the roving camera and the zoom lens, which can give a multiplicity of viewpoints and close-ups of the most intricate operations.

Thus the form of a communication should exercise the mind of the author as much as the content. Mere description, the bald statement of fact, is not enough. However accurate and explicit a description may be, it imposes a burden on the mind of the receiver unless given some human significance. If the receiver wishes to assimilate the content, the information, he has to do the same work as the author all over again; he receives no help in identifying the role that the information can play in enlarging his view of the world and his ability to cope. The creative imagination of the author supplies this help. By the use of the creative imagination we can enhance the understanding of human experience, and transform the experience of the individual into an experience of general human significance. A great author transcends time and space; as Ben Jonson said, Shakespeare is not of one age, but for all time. Each successive generation comes to such works, not simply for information in the sense of factual data (which is often wrong), but for insight into the human condition.

Such insight has above all the quality of permanence. The physical world in which we live changes very little in terms of human chronology. The struggle to master the environment and make it tolerable to live in faces every generation. Only the tools and the techniques change and improve our capacity for understanding the struggle and achieving a degree of mastery. The more we can build on the knowledge and understanding of previous generations, the less we have to do their work all over again. Hence the danger of too much reliance on those media of communication which have no intrinsic permanence. The News on the radio or television screen is heard, seen, and gone, unless recorded in some additional form for storage and future consultation — as a book may store a series of lectures. Consultation of a computer file on a visual display unit is equally ephemeral; continuous consultation is much more easily done by means of a printout on paper. In itself, the permanent record, on film, tape, or disc, is invisible to the naked eye, and can only be consulted through a machine.

Naturally, some information has only temporary value: booking a seat in a theatre or an aeroplane, performing a complex calculation as part of a scientific experiment or a financial transaction, and so forth. On reflection, I am inclined to pause even over the second example: the notebooks of eminent scientists are among the prized possessions of libraries lucky enough to have them, precisely because they form a permanent record of the work and thought that led along the path to eminence, a chronicle of achievement.

The need for permanent storage facilities are well recognized, as the often-heard phrase 'keep that because it may come in useful' testifies. The place of libraries in such facilities is also well recognized; many important or wealthy people have built or benefited libraries. The Bodleian Library in Oxford spent large sums of money to acquire original Shakespeare Quartos which the good Sir Thomas discarded as ephemera, and several Presidents of the United States have made elaborate provision for ensuring that their working papers are preserved for posterity. The techniques of library and archive science, like every other technique, grow and develop, and the professional philosophy of librarians and archivists develops likewise.

There are different kinds of library and their methods and activities vary. But they all rest on three major functions: assembling, or building, a collection of the records of information, of all types; providing a catalogue, or index, to the collection; and providing access to the collection in order to ensure that it serves a useful social purpose.

The great national and university libraries above all have devoted themselves to collection building; the concept owes much to the idealism, energy and organizing ability of two great librarians of the nineteenth century, Sir Antony Panizzi at the British Museum and Herbert Putnam at the Library of Congress. Panizzi set up the goal for the British Museum – the best collection of material on Great Britain, and the best on every other country outside its own borders; generations of scholars have borne witness to his wisdom, and though the bright vision has somewhat faded, the complex of institutions known as the British Library has probably a wider impact on society at large.

Collection building depends on scholarship, knowledge of subjects and their bibliography, and the care and preservation of documents. Through these scholarly activities, librarians in academic libraries have for centuries carefully collected and looked after the documents and records of the societies in which they lived. Such records form the very foundation of our civilization. We call those centuries from which few records remain, the 'Dark Ages'; we call those centuries which saw the rediscovery of the Greeks and Romans, through their books, the 'Renaissance' – the rebirth of learning.

When, also in the nineteenth century, the founding of public libraries began to spread throughout Europe and the United States, they brought with them the concept of free access to their collections for the general public. That readers of all levels of society should have the opportunity freely to consult the records of civilization was something of a quiet revolution, and came not without protest. Herbert Spencer no more approved of free libraries than of free bakeries. Open access required a sensible organization or classification of the books on the shelves; users of the public libraries, unlike most users of academic libraries, wanted to study subjects but often did not know the names of the authors of likely books.

The two World Wars and the subsequent years brought a spectacular growth in libraries serving science and industry. Since speed and accuracy of service was of the essence, reference service developed into information service. The librarian became the information officer, a member of the research team who had the specific duty, not only of collecting, but also of sending information to his colleagues without waiting for them to ask. He had to know about the fields of work of the laboratories and the factories, to identify and obtain quickly all new work that would have relevance to those fields.

Every library inherits these three great responsibilities. In so far as a library takes the positive role of dissemination, it deserves the name of 'Information Service', and forms an essential part of the cultural infrastructure called for by the Conference on Cultural Policies. The conference also considered that 'in order to come to full flower, both science and technology, and culture require complete freedom, guaranteeing and stimulating creativity and invention'. To bring these aspirations to reality requires greater understanding of the psychological foundations of the communications process, and of the roles and values of the organs which society sets up to promote it.

Chapter 3

COMMUNICATION AND SOCIETY

Society recognizes that communication is a social process by establishing systems for achieving it. Most of these are planned by one organization or another, but some come into being as a result of informal arrangements between people of similar interests who wish to keep in touch with one another. The origin of such systems, lost in the mists of time, certainly lay in the desire of those in power, usually kings or priests, to keep valuable information to themselves. Discoveries and observations like those of the Sumerians and Egyptians on the seasonal ebbs and floods of the great rivers, were either handed on orally or recorded in great secrecy. Aristotle relates how Thales of Miletos made a fortune through his knowledge of the stars: he predicted a good olive harvest and hired all the olive presses cheaply during the winter so that he could rent them out dearly when the harvest came.

The growth of market economies and international trade led to an increase in the use of records for commerce and business, and the invention of the papyrus roll and the codex form of book. But the view of knowledge as the right of only the elite persisted. In his life of Alexander, Plutarch records a letter that he wrote to his tutor while campaigning in Asia Minor: 'Alexander to Aristotle. Greeting. You have not done well to publish your books of oral doctrine. For what is there now that we excel others in, if those things which we have been particularly instructed in be laid open to all? For my part, I assure you, I had rather excel others in the knowledge of what is excellent, rather than in the extent of my power and dominion. Farewell'. Aristotle had already recognized the value of books for expounding a systematic treatise and a detailed argument that requires the reader to give serious study, with the possibility of continuous reference back and forth, from one part to another. It is fortunate for us that he did, for if the masters of the Greek and Roman cultures had not recorded their ideas in this way, there could have been no Renaissance in Europe at the end of the Middle Ages.

Although manuscripts were written and copied in a multitude of monasteries and scriptoria for circulation among scholars, the invention of printing saw the beginnings of the modern publishing industry. The pioneers, such as Caxton in England and Aldus Manutius in Italy, were scholars as well as craftsmen, and often combined in their own shops the trades of editor, printer, publisher and bookseller. Groups who formed themselves together for discussion and exchange of information had been known from antiquity, though they had not played any significant role in publishing. Some of these were informal, and peripatetic, like the Wandering Scholars, who were known throughout Europe for their popular and very secular Latin songs, *Carmina Burana*; others were more or less formally constituted in 'academies' like the Brethren of Sincerity at Basra in the tenth century and the Academia Secretarum Naturae in Naples in the sixteenth. The Arabs throughout the Middle East and in Spain set up translating offices which played a large part in preserving Greek and Latin literature and science.

Many colleges and libraries were founded, particularly by the Abbasid Caliphs, and were open to the general public. The esteem in which they were held is illustrated by the Caliph al-Mustansir who established a college in Baghdad in 1232 and appointed his son al-Mustasim as Librarian. When al-Mustasim succeeded to the Caliphate, he returned to inspect the Library, and finding its condition not to his satisfaction, he put the new librarians into prison for two days to induce them to do better.

The book, however, was not the only medium of communication. For the advance of science in particular, correspondence and the letter were equally important. Volumes of correspondence have always provided valuable source material for historians in all fields. In science, the particular character of the letter differed from that of the book, in that it did not form a systematic treatise, but rather a quick and easy way of communicating a new idea or experiment. The Scientific Revolution of the sixteenth and seventeenth centuries began the succession of formal organizations of like-minded scholars which has lasted to our own time. These groups converted into a formal institution what had previously existed as a sometimes haphazard exchange between a few friends.

Such were the group of scholars, or *virtuosi*, who began to meet in London in the 1640s, men of 'capacious and searching spirits' who called themselves a Philosophical College, and were nicknamed 'The Invisibles' by Robert Boyle. Meeting sometimes in a tavern, sometimes at Gresham College, and later in Oxford, they were inspired by the love of knowledge rather than by hope of gain, and like their great predecessor, Francis Bacon, they took all knowledge as their province as well as their own particular field. In 1662, they became the Royal Society.

The membership of the 'Royal' originally included artists and men of letters as well as men of science. Dryden, Waller and Wren were members, and Thomas Sprat, historian of the Society and later Bishop of Rochester wrote that 'their intention was more, to communicate to each other, their discoveries ... than a united, constant, or regular inquisition'. They were encouraged to write about their work, not in the high-flown esoteric 'language of wits and scholars' but in plain and simple English which corresponded to natural speech. The same qualities can be seen in the writing of one of the great founders of Russian science, M V Lomonosov, of whom Pushkin wrote that his style 'springs mainly from his deep knowledge of the literary Slavonic language, and from a happy fusion of the latter with the language of the common people'.

The letter as a means of communication gave rise to the periodical, though the Royal Society was not the first to publish a periodical, even in England. News and comment on political events had begun to circulate before the Civil War, but the *Philosophical transactions* was the first scientific periodical to have had a continuous existence down to the present day. *The weekly memorials for the ingenious*, first published in 1682, was the forerunner of the modern abstracting and indexing journal. The seventeenth century saw that wide proliferation of periodical publications which cover not only the interests of research scientists and scholars, but also the educated 'gentleman' who read *The tatler, The spectator*, and Johnson's *The rambler*. Societies were set up by the professions: lawyers, doctors, engineers and many others whose main aims were to provide a forum for discussion and a vehicle for communication between the members.

Commercial publishers, who had handled the book trade since the invention of printing, also moved into the periodical field, first with the literary and political journals, but later in specialist fields of scholarship and science; among the outstanding examples are the *The economist*, founded in 1843, and *Nature* founded in 1869 and still published by the house of Macmillan. *Nature* was begun, as its early issues show, as an attempt to communicate advances in science to a wider readership, and such a collaboration of scholars and businessmen for the purpose of disseminating information has often been repeated.

The great intellectual and industrial revolution brought about by the advent of the electronic computer, has intensified all the problems of formal communication methods. Many factors have contributed, some of which have been with us much longer — the great increase in the numbers of people engaged in research in all fields, who want to publish because in many cases their careers depend on their list; the consequent growth in the size of the publishing industry; the improvement of transport facilities which have made it possible for international scholarship to develop as much through meetings, conferences, sabbatical leave, as through the regular periodicals and books.

While none of these factors can now be thought of as new, the size of their growth has led to a radically different situation, in which systems of communication which are long established and have stood the test of time are being subjected to critical scrutiny and revaluation. Techniques like systems analysis, derived from General System Theory, have developed as a result of the need to make step-by-step breakdowns of any process if it is to benefit from automation. In the institutions of communication, this has meant a direct challenge to the use of print by electronic means of transmitting information. On the one hand, the instant availability made possible by satellite transmission not only brings the news as it happens, but also provides access to colleagues across the world by electronic mail; conferences and business meetings by television links are now a common feature in the multinational corporations, so that decisions can be reached immediately without recourse to the postal service or even the telephone. On the other hand, the storage capacity of even microcomputers is now so great that vast quantities of information, including bibliographical data, can be consulted in far less time than by a search through even the best compendia, such as *Chemical abstracts*. At present, the sale of printed sources like this provides the income necessary to support the compilation and dissemination through on-line access, but estimates from usually sober and reliable sources forecast that in a decade or two a significant proportion of specialist periodicals will appear only in electronic form.

An analysis of the systems which society organizes for the transmission of information shows that they fall into three major groups, each of which has two phases: production and publication; collection and arrangement; dissemination and use. The use of information begins the cycle all over again, and leads to the production of more new information, more new literature available for collection.

In speaking of production and publication, we refer, in fact, to an individual who decides that he has something to add to the common stock of publicly available information, and therefore wishes to communicate with others who are likely to share his interest. If he knew them all personally, presumably correspondence would offer a direct route, and no doubt this will become less of a tiresome chore when at least his friends will all have access to an electronic mail terminal. Some years ago, an abortive attempt to revive communication by letter through Exchange Groups came to nothing, rousing considerable hostility among editors and secretaries of learned societies, who saw these groups as a threat to their traditional journals, newsletters and conference publications. The Exchange Groups, being based on print, were unable at the time to escape from the institutions of publication. But direct dialogue between comuputer terminals successfully breaks out of those bounds, and bypasses the formal channels.

This may have the undesirable effect of further concentrating access to new information in new invisible colleges whose members use invisible means of communication, and all know one another. The unknown colleagues, who are in touch through their participation in the formal institutions — membership of the same societies, subscription to the same journals — may find that they are suddenly excluded from professional discussions which they expect as one of the benefits derived from the institution.

The situation has dangers even for the established scholar who automatically belongs to the Invisibles. As a user of information himself, as a consumer, he also profits from the activities of the institution because he too learns about the work of people who are unknown to him. This aspect is particularly important for younger scholars who may be at the beginning of their research and hope to bring it to the attention of senior colleagues. This has great importance for society in that they will be the leaders of tomorrow. As yet, they do not sit on the important committees, meet regularly with those in the seats of power, and influence the way that their particular field of work develops.

Electronic dialogue also raises the question of assessment. The formal institutions provide channels along which information flows in a recognized and socially accepted way. At certain points, information comes under scrutiny and judged on its fitness to be passed on. Learned societies send the papers submitted to them to 'referees' who have an established reputation and can be relied on to maintain standards. Such assessors have also come to be called 'gatekeepers', who can open or close the channel for any particular item of information. As McGarry points out in a detailed discussion of this role, 'The editor of a newspaper or journal is a gatekeeper, so also is the producer of our nightly news bulletins'.

This question of assessment is crucial. In the present publishing system, when an author decides to make his work public, he submits it to the informed judgement of established colleagues who have claims to be thought of as experts. The very fact of publication in a recognized journal or through a reputable publisher guarantees that the work has reached an acceptable standard. Even without the problems posed by electronic transmission, the situation has reached a crisis. The steady increase in the number of books and journals published can be interpreted as a sign of healthy growth, but there is an unfortunate side-effect in the over-production of information.

The symptoms which we should be guarding against include: a lowering of standards where gatekeepers are bypassed; much duplicate publishing of the same article in different places; excessive publishing of ephemeral 'news'; the proliferation of commonplace 'Notes' or 'Letters to the Editor'. Reliance on the market in an era when funds are plentiful does not guarantee quality in the article for sale.

Publication for an author means introducing him to a social group who work in a specialized field and who wish to establish formal links with others, known and unknown, in the same field. The publisher acts as a sponsor in so far as he has a system of assessment, and so far the peer group has proved to be the favoured system. The final judgement rests with society itself, whether the work becomes part of the paradigm, achieving what Ziman calls 'consensibility', or whether it proves to be so seminal as to effect a scientific revolution.

Here begins the process of collection and arrangement, which introduces another part of the social organization; librarians, documentalists, information officers. These are among the many names attached to those who have the responsibility of ensuring that the output of the publishing process comes to rest in places where it can easily be consulted and put to use. It is not enough for a work to be published; it must become publicly available if it is to enter into the common stock of knowledge. Francis Bacon already saw the necessity, and the value, of such collectors in forming the riches of Solomon's House, the research institute of New Atlantis: 'For the several employments and offices of our fellows, we have twelve ... who bring us the books and abstracts, and patterns of experiments of all other parts. These we call "merchants of light"'.

This group plays an essential role in the communication process, even though its value at times seems to be ignored. Librarians and information officers go on devising and elaborating systems for organizing the published literature, while users fail to comprehend or even realize the existence of these systems. This all too often results in re-inventing the bibliographical wheel, meeting all the same problems and coming up with solutions that have been superseded but are claimed to be revolutionary. It emphasizes again the need for better communication among the communicators.

The social function of these merchants consists of collecting, arranging and disseminating the information that has been made publicly available. This first appears in primary forms — books, pamphlets, periodicals, and a mass of 'grey' literature which does not enter the formal channels but which achieves circulation none the less. Secondary records also need to be acquired, and in some libraries created: indexes, abstracts, surveys of the literature. This bibliographical apparatus acts as a map of a subject field; it is not the field itself, but consists of a series of access points by means of which the user can enter and study the field. The modern librarian, as specialist in information handling, has to know the sources and establish the necessary routines for getting them into his library.

Once there, they must be organized and arranged by systems of cataloguing and classification. In the days when the user of a library was expected to know the names of writers whose works he needed, catalogues of authors' names gave adequate access: the British Museum's General Catalogue of Printed Books is a monument to this approach, and many years of highly specialized discussions have produced a series of Anglo-American Cataloguing Rules. With the highest professional motives, the compilers of these Rules have laboured to make provision for every possible variant and element in a catalogue entry. Correct forms of names for complicated documents like government and other institutional documents; reports of committees which have a specific name and title but are commonly known by the name of the chairman; conference proceedings; and so on, until one almost forgets that most publications have an author whose name appears on the title page, and whose work bears the name he gave it.

It may be that the cost of storing detailed cataloguing entries in machine-readable form will call into question the desirability of treating every document as if it were a unique incunable from the cradle days of printing. If this is so, we should remember all the same that, while brevity is the soul of wit, an ideal form before us lets us know what we are doing if we decide to retreat from it. The Anglo-American Cataloguing Rules, firmly based on principles reached by international discussion, provide such an ideal form and serve as an international standard of high repute.

Classification, arrangement by subject in libraries, has to put into systematic order the literature that is actually written, and many systems have been invented for the purpose. Probably the best known is the Decimal Classification of Melvil Dewey, and its offspring, the Universal Decimal Classification now sponsored by the International Federation for Documentation, and published in English by the British Standards Institution. The pioneering nature of Dewey's scheme ensured its popularity, but despite its nineteen editions and an office for revisions in the Library of Congress, it has failed to keep up with the progress of knowledge, mainly because its basis in nineteenth century thought patterns makes it difficult to introduce sufficient flexibility to cope with the complexities of the modern publishing output.

Dewey's contribution was revolutionary in its time, when the first slim edition came out in 1876. He saw clearly two fundamental problems: to arrange books on shelves by a relative location of subjects; and to mechanize the relative order by means of an expansible notation into which new subjects could be inserted at appropriate places. The first he solved by adopting the technique of the classificatory sciences and dividing subjects from genus to species; the second by attaching to his array of subjects arabic numbers divided by the decimal principle.

In addition to this analytical approach, Dewey introduced a synthetic feature. Where a subject could be divided by historical or geographical treatment — 'Birds of California', for example — he did not list all the possible subdivisions but instructed the user to add the notation from the Class History, which included Geography and Description. The user of the scheme, he said, 'will notice this mnemonic principle in several hundred places in the classification, and will find it of great practical utility in numbering and finding books'.

This synthetic principle has been greatly elaborated in the Universal Decimal Classification, and in the second edition of the Bibliographic Classification first devised by H E Bliss. The most detailed theoretical study was made by S R Ranganathan, whose Colon Classification was originally produced for the library of Madras University. Ranganathan proposed that all the divisions of any major subject, or Main Class, could be related to one or other of five Fundamental Categories based on the concepts of Time, Space, Energy, Matter, and what he named Personality. Time and Space clearly relate to historical and geographical subdivision. Energy or motion and Matter are well-recognized physical concepts of Things and Processes. Personality he found hard to define except to say that it represented Wholeness, end products, the main focus of attention in any class. It can easily be related to the similar concept of wholes or entities in General System Theory. This process of division he called Facet Analysis, and it has proved invaluable to all subsequent compilers of classification schemes and subject analyses.

The notion of fundamental categories can also be found in Aristotle, and in Roget's *Thesaurus of English words and phrases*, which uses abstractions like Relation, Quantity, Number, Space, Matter, Sentient and Moral Powers, for the purpose of arranging concepts into categories 'to facilitate the Expression of Ideas and to assist in Literary Composition'.

Cataloguing and classification are the tools for achieving systematic arrangement, but classification, as one of the basic mental processes for organizing thought, also helps in the dissemination processes. These involve techniques for steering information to those who can use it. It may take the long-established form of reference service, in which a librarian will use his knowledge of sources to guide an enquirer to the answer to his question, or it may be a system of Selective Dissemination of Information as a regular despatch of new acquisitions to those users whose field of interest they cover. Reference service is exactly what its name implies: looking up a subject in any book, pamphlet, periodical in order to provide information to fill a gap in the knowledge of an enquirer, of which he has become conscious. 'Do you have anything on so-and-so?' is a question asked of every librarian at some time or other in his career. SDI service, on the other hand, does not form a response to such a question. The librarian sets up a series of 'profiles', descriptions of the interests of users of the service, and he examines new acquisitions to see whether the information they contain matches any of these profiles. Where it does, where there is a 'hit', a note is sent to the person or persons identified. If this person is very important, such as a director of research, or a city councillor, the item itself may be sent. Generally speaking, however, an SDI note may take one of three forms. It may be a single note to a specific person with a specialized interest; it may be a list of items for a group, such as a university faculty, or a particular laboratory; it may be a copy of the contents page of a periodical just received, to go either to an individual or to a group. The last not only tells the recipient what are the contents of the latest issue, it also reminds him that the issue has arrived in the library, so a visit there will not be wasted.

The new technology has a stimulating effect on all three of these groups of processes. This applies at the sociological level as much as at the technical. Technically, the way forward means making the best possible use of the now easily available machines for handling large quantities of data, but this must be in the light of the needs of users, and not of the aspirations of computer manufacturers. Despite the efforts of the Library of Congress and the British Library, we have not yet discovered the most efficient and economical way of using centrally produced cataloguing data from the MARC project for machine-readable catalogues.

In the Soviet Union, authority resides in central institutions such as the All-Union Institute for Scientific and Technical Information, VINITI, with its impressive range of primary and secondary publications and depth of research into the use of automation for their production. Other institutions in Moscow and in other countries of Eastern Europe have followed this lead and established centralized bibliographical systems. In the United States, the National Academy of Sciences and the National Science Foundation have for a long time tried to stimualte co-operation and co-ordination as well as competition. The Institute for Scientific Information in Philadelphia has made a great theoretical as well as a practical contribution with its Citation Indexes which now cover the whole field of knowledge. In Britain, the Minister for Arts and Libraries has a Library and Information Services Council to advise him, and includes LISC reports in the Annual Report which he makes to Parliament.

On the international scene, a great number and variety of technical and general organizations concern themselves with communication. The list of countries and organizations attending the two Unesco conferences in 1982 gives a fair idea of the range. Learned societies, through their own organizations such as the International Council of Scientific Unions, ICSU, have also contributed and shown great sensitivity to criticism and willingness to modify their systems in response to the comments of users. For future planning, the UNISIST project of Unesco and the General Information Programme represent a power base from which an integrated system may be managed, and the system of national committees, like the Unesco National Commissions themselves, ensure that member states have plenty of opportunity to influence progress.

What I find disturbing is the resolute opposition on the

part of the GIP to widen its role by co-operating with, for example, the International Programme for the Development of Communication. The GIP has good relations with international bodies in the field of libraries and archives – the International Federation of Library Associations, the International Federation for Documentation, the International Council on Archives. It works well with other specialized agencies such as the International Standards Organization, the International Atomic Energy Authority, the United Nations Industrial Development Organization; most of these are based in science and technology.

But no man is an island, and no subject can remain pure and uncontaminated by others. Despite all efforts to conceal it, the ugly truth of the matter is that science and technology are just as much affected by political considerations as any other branch of culture. Hiding from this will not make it go away; and if we wish to improve international understanding and promote peaceful co-operation, then all organizations concerned with information must learn to work together towards the common goal. The history of planned and unplanned, formal and informal, methods of communication shows that Aristotle, and not Alexander, made the most enduring impact on the advancement of learning and its beneficent effect on such human progress as we have so far managed to achieve. Library and information services make their own unique contribution to creativity and the advancement of learning, and international communication stands to benefit greatly from this contribution.

Chapter 4

INFORMATION AND THE PSYCHOLOGY OF USERS

The study of human psychology has increased vastly in recent decades, but little attention goes to the psychology of the users of library and information services. This is not altogether surprising: psychologists are not noted for their inclination to apply their science to themselves, and the extensive series of investigations carried out for the American Psychological Association have been sociological rather than psychological. Librarians have lately become concerned with what is, perhaps somewhat arrogantly, termed 'user education', and the Library and Information Services Council itself has commissioned a working party to report. A great deal of research and documentation goes on at the Department of Library and Information Studies at Loughborough University and the Centre for User Studies at Sheffield University.

On the whole, though, this work also tends to look at organizational questions from the viewpoint of librarians and information specialists, preoccupied mainly with the analysis of their own systems rather than with the psychology of their users. At the City University, N J Belkin sets out the problem as 'facilitating the effective communication of desired information between human generator and human user', and while his approach stems mainly from mathematical theories of information transfer, he also notes that, at least by implication, information scientists are concerned with 'information in human, cognitive communication systems'.

The fruitful application of General System Theory to

library and information services takes into account not only the organizational problems of collection, arrangement and dissemination within the system itself. It involves looking at the super-systems, the community of users, and the ways in which they come to have a need for information. The case for doing so has been memorably stated by Ziman: 'a laboratory without a library is like a decorticated cat: the motor activities continue to function, but lack co-ordination of memory and purpose'.

Like the managers of any institution, librarians have to consider the service as a thing-in-itself, an integrated whole, in order to devise efficient methods for securing the harmonious working together of all the parts. But the shape of the service as a whole, the relative importance of the various parts, must be determined by the way in which the service relates to its community of users, the outside world. For the public library, this consists of those who live and work in the local area; for the university, the students and faculty members; for the special library, the members of the institute or industry, whether in scientific or commercial departments.

The sociological aspects of this inter-system relation are of the first importance. An over-emphasis on the mathematical style of analysis was corrected by A I Mikhailov and his colleagues at VINITI in their classic paper on what they called 'Informatics'. This name has not been without ambiguity, since it also has a wide currency in Western Europe with the meaning of computer theory. The importance of Mikhailov's paper lies in the stress he lays on the social role of the library information service. The realization or practice of this role comes from the interaction of the service with its individual users pursuing their own individual aims. These are of course shaped by the communities and organization within which the users live and work. Each library makes its own contribution towards these communities through the help it gives to the members. The individual members are the foundation of a community, its part or sub-systems, and their relationships to the community and to each other, makes the community work and in turn secures their own progress.

Individual human progress, in fact, depends very much on this relationship between institutions of society and people. The individuals, as parts of a social system, belong to it by virtue of their being themselves, the persons they are; it is for this reason that they have value for the system, and membership of it has value for them. They have, as themselves, their own personal integrity, the organization of their bodies and minds that constitutes their personality. It is the task of psychology to study these internal relationships.

But just as we cannot justify a claim to be using systems analysis so long as we remain content to look at libraries as static units in isolation from their communities of users, so we cannot reduce user psychology to the study of Man in isolation from society. We all live in, and are parts of, an evolving, dynamic world. But before we can fully interpret the relations between Man and community we have to stand back from the real world and consider each in turn. Frederick Engels pointed out a century ago, in his polemic against Eugen Dühring, the sterility of falling into the metaphysical way of thinking, 'the habit of considering objects and processes in isolation, detached from the whole vast interconnexion of things; nevertheless, in order to form an adequate conception of things, we have of course to study them in detail', and this means that 'in order to understand these details, we must detach them from their natural and historical connexions, and examine each one separately'.

We must, however, beware also of falling into the behaviourist way of thinking, and studying users only as individual stimuli to librarians. This often happens: the user is regarded somewhat as a black box, and instead of studying the internal working of his mind, we pay attention only to those outward and visible signs of his mental activity as they appear to affect librarians and their activity. This is to study librarian psychology rather than user psychology. In looking at user psychology, we must, for the moment, detach him from the end result of his activity, his connection with the library, and study him as an individual in his own terms. What is his milieu? What are his aims? How does he come to have a need for information? What does he think he is doing when he consults a library?

This may very well differ somewhat from what we as observers think he is doing. Those who make enquiries in libraries are notoriously vague in their statements of need, not surprisingly indeed, when we reflect that what has brought them to this point is that they have become aware of a gap in their information. Even when the event has what we might think of as a trivial character — a request for light fiction, for instance — nevertheless the motive for making the request is basically the same. Even light fiction has been produced by authors who consider that they have a view of the world which they would like to communicate to others in order to enhance their understanding of that particular view.

We have, then, to cease considering the library user as part of the management or bibliographical system, and remind ourselves that the library exists to satisfy the needs of users, and not the other way about.

There are several facets to examine when considering the ways in which users relate to libraries as providers of information, in its broadest sense as statements made by individuals about concepts they have assimilated and which add up to a point of view. In order to lay stress on the relation between librarianship and user psychology, I shall use the technique of facet analysis in the Ranganathan manner, and look in turn at Personality, Matter, Energy. We have already looked at Personality in discussing the thought processes that go on in the minds of authors and producers of information who wish to present an ordered and coherent account of some part of the world they live in for the benefit of others. The other side of the medal displays the thought processes that go on in the minds of those whose mental picture lacks, to a greater or lesser extent, some element of that ordered and coherent structure.

Miles of library shelving are occupied by attempts to lay bare the thought processes that go on in arriving at a decision to take some course of action, but most modern psychologists, sociologists, linguists, and similar theoreticians view them as an attempt to enlarge an existing structure of concepts so as to improve understanding of the human environment and live a more satisfying life. This does not mean merely mastering the physical aspects of the world, though this is basic. It means also acquiring a fuller understanding of the human condition, a deeper sympathy for our fellow beings and the predicaments they find themselves in; from this, we acquire, consciously or unconsciously, a fuller understanding of ourselves. This makes it obvious that information services should not confine themselves to science and technology, as the GIP seems to prefer. There is ample scope for similar methods to improve communication in the social sciences and humanities, and bring about a higher level of understanding and insight as well as larger stores of bits of information.

We have to apply ourselves to the question, how does an individual form concepts and organize them into a coherent pattern, and how does he go about setting up this organization? Bentley Glass put his finger on the nub of the matter in his John Dewey Society Lecture on the 'timely' — empirical knowledge used in our daily relations with society — and the 'timeless' — the whole range of human values that have become Man's ideals as a result of our long evolutionary development. Glass says: 'The data and the facts alone do not constitute knowledge in the sense of understanding. Information is useful, but the observations must be fitted into concepts and conceptual schemes, or paradigms, that determine our outlook and direct our processes of investigation and enquiry ... What is necessary is insight, and insight may come through learning, if we study the right things in the right way'.

So far there has not appeared a great deal of this type of study in the literature of library and information science; and, to return the compliment, we do not find much about library and information services in the literature of psychology, not even in the surveys of the American Psychological Association. Here, as in relation with others involved in communication, is a gulf which should be bridged.

We shall not bridge this gap if we rely only on the method adopted by the charitable Quen-Ki-Tong, in the account given by the story-teller Kai Lung of the wedding between the valiant Liao and the beautiful Ts'ain: 'In the most commodious chamber of the house the elegant wedding gifts are conspicuously displayed; let us stand beside the one which we have contributed, and point out its excellence to those who pass by'. On the contrary, we shall only be able to show the excellence of our library service if it can be seen by the user to have direct significance for his own thought processes, and not as an exhibit to be admired and even wondered at.

Fortunately the process of learning how to form concepts has been studied both widely and in depth, and is of course closely related to what goes on in the mind of an author when presenting his point of view to the public. The works of many writers, such as J P Guilford in the United States, Jean Piaget in Switzerland, L S Vygotsky and A R Luria in the Soviet Union, Liam Hudson in Britain, as well as many other experimental psychologists, all show that concepts do not come into the mind fully formed, nor are we equipped with some innate mental mechanism, permanent and unchanging, by means of which we not only can, but must, process sense data in one particular way. It has been shown many times that each individual comes to transform the percepts and information he receives, whether by direct experience or through a source such as a book, a periodical, or a chat at the bar, into his forms of knowledge in his own way by means of his own activities. Since the history of the activities of each individual is unique to him, each individual is himself unique, and this uniqueness extends to each individual's store of knowledge. None of us knows exactly the same as another.

Nor, in the learning process, is information inscribed on a child's mind, as *tabula rasa*; failure to learn is no longer generally attributed to mere idleness or to hatred of the teacher. We learn to form concepts by actively operating on the world around us, by experimenting, by putting things in order and classifying them, by observing differences between things and the ways they behave. Both Piaget and Vygotsky have emphasized that awareness of differences precedes awareness of similarities. By acquiring the skills of dividing and grouping, we learn to classify and to predict, and from this we go on to the realization that we can learn from the experience of others as well as our own. We do not have to carry out every experiment ourselves: we can read what someone else says about it, because if it comes within a class of phenomena we already know, we understand what we read. This forms the basis of claims for the value of library services to society: information gained from reading may be second-hand, but it is none the less valid for that.

Percepts derived from experience, and information derived from records, are integrated into a coherent pattern in the mind by being processed into becoming part of an organized structure of notions. They are transformed from what Vygotsky calls 'spontaneous concepts', immediately perceived in isolation, into 'scientific concepts' assimilated into a pre-existing pattern of thought. When Pasteur said that chance favours the prepared mind, he meant that such a pre-existing pattern prepares the way for the entry of new information so that it falls into place appropriately and with significance. The Princes of Serendip were so successful in taking in what chance offered that they gave the useful word 'serendipity' to our vocabulary.

These pre-existing patterns of thought, rather like a jigsaw puzzle, have an integrity of their own, even if they are incomplete: the parts fit together and make up a picture which adds to our satisfaction. New pieces increase that satisfaction, for unlike the completed jigsaw, our patterns of thought are always capable of improvement by the addition of new experience and new information. Bronowski's thesis suggests that Man is part of the Nature, but is different from automata in that every person, though made up of the same set of chemicals, has a unique personality by virtue of a unique experience. Each self, a personality, grows by enhancement through experience, and this human ability to grow through experience, whether directly through the senses, or indirectly through the recorded experience of others, forms a corner-stone in the edifice of creativity.

Creativity, in art or in science, consists in the ability to present information in a light which had not appeared before, but which nevertheless adds to a coherent pattern already publicly available. As Medawar says, 'that "creativity" is beyond analysis is a romantic illusion we must now outgrow'. It may be found in a new way of presenting familiar information, as, for example, a new interpretation of a Shakespeare play or a Beethoven symphony. In science, new information may enlarge and consolidate the existing paradigm, or may give a satisfactory explanation for the discrepancies and tensions, and lead to a break with the past and a new paradigm. An information service should provide an account of the paradigm and the discrepancies.

The judgement of creativity, furthermore, depends on the extent to which it is communicable. A paradigm cannot be overturned except by public consensus, because it does not rest on inspired guesswork but on hard work accumulating the details and recording them for others to verify or, in Popper's thesis, to falsify. The essence of creativity is that it communicates the enhancement of the self to others; it makes them more aware of the significance of phenomena for themselves, and not simply for the creative person. The 'mute, inglorious Miltons' in Thomas Gray's village were inglorious precisely because they were mute.

The user of a library aims to enlarge his own store of information, and his own understanding of the world, by a more or less purposeful search for what others have said that will make a significant improvement to his knowledge, the structure of thought already existing in his mind. If the new information achieves this, it will have added permanent value, and will remain in the memory.

This brings us to the second facet in this discussion, the Matter facet. Ranganathan called a library an externalized memory precisely because the documents and records in it save the time and the mind of a user by giving him easy access to information which he would otherwise have to remember himself. We do not wish to clutter our minds with every item of information we learn, in case it may come in useful. A railway timetable, a table of constants, a dictionary of quotations, will save a good deal of memory space and allow us to discriminate about what we shall remember ourselves.

A librarian's role includes the arrangement of these documents so that they present the maximum possible relevance to the several areas of public knowledge. We may not, as librarians, be called upon to evaluate the worth of any particular document, though our opinions may well be worth considering. But we are very much concerned with the assessment of relevance: the place of any information in relation to its subject field, and the extent to which it may be pertinent to the needs of one particular user. The making of abstracts, indexes, surveys, aims to provide users with what they need in a convenient and easily assimilable form.

The modern library is an organization of great complexity, because of the great volume and variety of the documentation with which it has to deal. Particularly for the new or inexperienced user, it may present a daunting spectacle, and its catalogues and classification schemes should be made to mitigate this impression. The computer makers realize this, and use the evocative term 'user friendly' to denote this quality of simplicity and ease of operation.

When we come to the Energy facet, we are in a somewhat different situation. In so far as it relates to production and publication, librarians may become involved with editorial work, and may well be able to offer useful advice to authors on some questions of presentation; style, layout citation of references, and the general mechanics rather than individual psychology.

What concerns us here, however, is the effort which a user is prepared to put into using the library and taking advantage of the services it offers. This depends on the extent of his motivation. A dread of apathy on the part of users haunts the minds of librarians and the professional press. And it is undoubtedly true that natural indolence works far more against satisfying the needs of the mind than of the body. But we can at least identify some of these needs and consider how a user may come to call upon documentation to help satisfy them.

The first, and probably the most serious, is the need to form habits of thinking that will enable the user to deal with the data provided by his senses. An education system aims to meet this need. There is indeed some truth in the old saying that a man's education is what he has left when he has forgotten everything he learned at school, because it emphasizes the fact that education does not mean merely committing vast and ever-increasing quantities of data to memory and testing success by examinations. It means developing the growing mind by providing significant experience to transform it into a precision instrument able to cope with the problems we encounter in every day life. For the truly creative person, it means imparting a sufficiently full picture of the paradigm to enable him to spot the discrepancies and devise explanations for resolving them.

Through our education, we get to know the details of natural phenomena, the facts of the case; we form concepts by incorporating these details into a structure that makes sense to us, and by this activity we attain to a mastery of this particular skill. We form habits of thought and speech which enable us to cope with the world and not be continually surprised by what happens every day. Having acquired this skill, we develop the incentive to use it: information is the material we use it on. It comes to us as our own sense data or as the record of what a writer has considered making publicly available, and we recognize the information as belonging to some mental picture we have, and which we now see as incomplete.

We may, or we may not, have known that our picture was incomplete. In the first case, we seek to remedy the lack, and become users of libraries and documents, or go to the laboratory to test a hypothesis; reference service aims to meet this case. In the second case, the library meets the need where it offers a selective dissemination of information service to provide its users with current awareness of what goes on in their fields of interest.

Like any other skill, the skill to use new information requires practice to keep it in trim, so that institutions which aim to provide information are an essential feature in the lives of the people, to consolidate their education and improve their culture. Libraries are no less important in this than newspapers, radio and television; all are elements in the same great process and stand to improve their own performance by co-operating and acknowledging their interdependence.

Skills also require rest and relaxation. For this reason, libraries have an important function in recreation. By this I mean, literally, re-creation, that refreshment and restoration of the human spirit which is essential if the mind is to continue to function positively, if it is not to become jaded, negative, uninspired, apathetic. This area of human need is pre-eminently the province of literature and the arts, and provision for it rests particularly with the public library in the local community.

The aim to arouse in the user's mind the motivation to use a library as a means of satisfying the need for continuing education, information and recreation must impose on the library above all the duty to demonstrate easy and easily identifiable access. I say 'demonstrate' rather than simply 'provide' because it seems to me that simple provision is not enough. All too often, users exhibit this symptom of 'apathy' because they either do not know of the library's existence, or they are unaware of the resources and services it can provide. Competence in the skills of information service must be accompanied by the homely qualities of nearness, comfort, a congenial atmosphere. Above all, the library service, which is developing new skills and new attitudes, must be seen to be doing so and fitting itself to play that essential part in the improvement of the quality of each individual's life which modern information resources offer and modern technology makes possible.

Chapter 5

KEEPERS AND FINDERS

If we affirm that a genuine need exists in modern society for intermediaries to make smooth the flow of information between its members; and if we maintain that librarians can and should qualify for inclusion in the company of specialists in communication; we should remember that the long and honourable tradition of 'keepers' and guardians of records has not only preserved information, but actually made civilized society attainable. The 'golden chain' of the Academy at Athens, as Raymond Irwin showed, lasted for a thousand years in a direct succession of teachers from Plato himself; and we can, Irwin goes on, 'by fair analogy adopt this term for the equally golden links that have handed on our tradition of scholarship and libraries from the beginnings of Western civilization in classical Athens to the present day ... the chain is there for all to see, both in human learning and in the books and libraries in which it is enshrined'. Princes, priests and poets have joined the profession; Casanova, Leibnitz, Goethe, Mao Zedong all were at one time pleased to call themselves 'librarian'.

The World Conference on Cultural Policies, asserting that each culture has a dignity and value which must be respected and preserved, recommended that Member States recognize the cultural values of different cultural groups, and encouraged them to preserve, develop and disseminate the culture of each group in all its many facets. Librarians, as keepers of the books, and abstracts, and patterns of experiments of all other parts, have played the major role in the precise task of preserving culture; in Matthew Arnold's phrase, the best that has been known and said in the world, including knowing what has been done in science and art as well as in letters.

Over the centuries, in the course of its historical development, the profession of librarian has made few, but significant, changes in its activities towards this end. The practice of the art responded to changing conditions in society at large, through the efforts of skilled practitioners sensitive to changing conditions and in harmony with the progress of their contemporary culture. The priests and kings were well aware that knowledge is power, and that the invention of writing actually gave them the means to transcend time and space by giving permanence to the information acquired and organized by wise men. Without these records, there could have been no development of civilization; each generation would remain in a primitive state because the lack of permanence meant no cumulation of information. Excavations among ancient civilizations show that the most ancient of all their records are in very permanent form indeed, carved on stone or clay tablets. Ironically, as technology advanced, the durability of the materials declined, and we have more trouble preserving the records of the nineteenth century AD than of the nineteenth century BC.

Considering the lack of a publishing industry, some of the libraries of antiquity were very large, but civilization progressed slowly; travel was difficult, access to information restricted to an elite, and communication between nations and cultures often meant confrontation in war rather than co-operation in peace. Greek science and culture took a thousand years to reach the Arabs, and even longer to help bring about the Renaissance in Europe. The impressive story of science and civilization in China remained virtually unknown in the West until very recently.

As keepers, librarians preserved the records and made them available on request, usually only to those with the right credentials. In any case, literacy was a rare skill, and still is in far too many countries. Professional concern was centred on the book as a physical object, even a thing of beauty, like the medieval manuscripts decorated to the extent that the decoration had a higher value than the contents. The Book of Kells was once regarded as the chiefest treasure of the Western World. Some documents are even today rightly regarded as objects of veneration: Magna Carta, the Declaration of Independence, the Lindisfarne Gospels; exhibitions displaying cultural history include documents as well as artefacts.

Because the tradition of learning was closely associated with individual wise men, as with Alexander and Aristotle, librarians desiring to promote access to their collections came to rely on the association of documents with particular names. In making lists and catalogues, arrangement by the names of writers has always occupied a pre-eminent place, the names of books – their titles – making an important accessory. Before the modern tendency to specialize and compartmentalize knowledge, a writer might range over many subjects in the same book, and take, like Bacon, all knowledge as his province. Thus the naming of subjects, and arrangement in classified order, was less precise and possibly less permanent than the naming of authors.

The invention of printing eventually brought about a degree of standardization in the physical aspects of book production, particularly of title pages. It took a long time; this can be seen by comparing title pages from successive centuries, from the detailed and often florid descriptions of the seventeenth and eighteenth centuries to the usually laconic and sometimes obscure sparseness of the present. One common feature persisted, however: the title page stated what the author wanted to call himself and his book. It contained a precise and more or less permanent name by means of which the book could be catalogued and found when wanted.

Such has been the preoccupation of librarians with this

admittedly vital means of identification that only during the last century have subject catalogues come into widespread use in libraries. Immense efforts have gone into the production of codes and standards for making entries in catalogues by the names of authors and titles of books. Codes and standards for entries by the names of subjects have had much less attention, and consequently are less widely accepted and used in making catalogues. Even today, some academic libraries have no subject catalogue, and the use of schemes of classification, which are systematic organizations of subjects, is rare in catalogues though taken for granted as the right way to arrange books on shelves.

It is not surprising, therefore, that many users and would-be users of libraries have the mistaken idea that librarians can only produce books, and information, if they are given the right name of an author. Because this establishes a direct link straight to the original producer of a document, it offers a quick and easy route to success in answering an enquiry. 'Who is it by?' tends to be a favourite riposte from a librarian anxious to find the quick and easy route. What we have to emphasize is that it is by no means the only route, and the broad and straight path can at times, even in a library, lead to destruction, of hope and of reputation.

Books, periodicals, reports, all the manifold types of document to be found in libraries, represent collections of statements made in a meaningful way by those who believe that they have something to say which will enlarge and improve the common store of information, and that their contribution will be sought for and welcomed by others. Each document contains some form of information, and the most obvious is indeed the name of the writer and the title he has given his work. The content of the work itself is of course what carries his message: his stock of information, or part of it at least, organized by its passage through his mind, and transformed, as far as he is able, into a form which fits what he has to say into a pattern which reflects reality as he understands it. He tries to communicate this understanding, and it is therefore the content, the subject, of his work that justifies its presence in a library. Even when a user looks for a particular author, it is because he knows that this author writes about an interesting subject.

This applies to literature as well as to science, even though works of literature do not necessarily convey the facts of the case, like *Hamlet* and the history of Denmark. But works of literature convey understanding and insight, and so have the same ultimate aim as works of science. We need to know the facts of life, so to speak, but we also need an enhanced consciousness of Man's place in Nature, and what we mean when we talk about a civilized way of life. The function of the original thinker, in any field, is to point out new facts and new relations and also to recognize their importance. In writing of 'The art of the physicist', Abdus Salam lays great stress on the fact that a revolutionary synthesis 'is achieved by some great physicist who goes through the spiritual agony of creation'. The creative writer looks for flaws in the paradigm, for gaps and inconsistencies in our general picture of reality.

Traditional library systems established to deal with the object in hand, which carried its own marks of identity fixed on it by its creator, were fine so long as users could be expected to know and ask for this correct name. And it often happens, especially in the humanities and in university libraries where students come armed with reading lists, some of which actually contain the proper identities of the works the students are supposed to read.

But it has long been obvious that when one comes up against a problem and starts looking for answers, one does not usually identify one particular author, but one particular subject, and even if one suspects that some author or other has written on it, one also wants to know about others. Sometimes the problem can be narrowed down to a specific datum, or 'bit' of information.

The modern library is perfectly capable of dealing with this type of enquiry. A subject classification scheme, even an outmoded scheme like Dewey's Decimal Classification, presents the universe of knowledge in an ordered sequence with related subjects adjacent to one another, so that a browse along the shelves should lead from what is already known to sources on the unknown. A properly constructed subject catalogue, like the *British national bibliography* does the same. The detailed subject index guides the user to an area of the classification where he finds his own subject in close proximity to those most closely related to it. A good faceted classification can even cope with new subjects and new relations in so far as the elements which go to make up complex subjects are not pre-coordinated into one relationship like that of genus to species in the classificatory sciences.

Finding information from the multitude of sources that are available today, whether visible on the shelves of libraries, or invisible in computer tapes and discs, depends on a variety of techniques that are the stock in trade of the modern librarian. It is not always, or even often, as simple as ABC; if it were, there would be no particular skills to acquire in education for the profession. Whereas the old librarians of renown knew their authors, and books on the making of libraries tended to give lists of the most eminent, the modern librarian must know authors, whose name is now legion, and also subjects, their bibliography, reference sources and what sort of material will suit readers.

He must know how to do a literature search, how to pursue the quarry through catalogues, encyclopaedias, indexes and abstracts. Most library users, even research workers, have only a sketchy notion, if indeed any notion at all, of how to search the literature to find subject information, and there is much to be said for some instruction in this particular skill to be given at least in secondary schools. A fairly simple routine can be followed, which will make a user feel at home in a library and give him a degree of confidence in using it efficiently.

The schedules of the classification scheme itself provide a guide to the area of the library shelves containing the books on a particular subject. Those who confine their interpretation of information to its narrowest sense of factual data seem to forget that browsing among the shelves of a good library provides a conspectus of any field of knowledge far wider than the compass of one individual mind, and offers a choice of approach and treatment which can lead to what W I B Beveridge calls a 'eureka situation'. Even a random juxtaposition of ideas gained by purposeful browsing may suddenly bring together apparently unconnected pieces of information to form a new, coherent picture, which is precisely what the enquirer looks for.

Even finding nothing suitable on the shelves via the scheme of classification does not mean that the library has failed to provide an answer; there are many reasons why this may be so. The right book may be on loan, at the bindery, in someone's office, or simply lost. The library catalogue will say if indeed the book is in stock. If the catalogue draws a blank, recourse may be had to a vast collection of printed catalogues and bibliographies, and indexes and abstracts guide users to the ever-increasing numbers of periodicals which, even in 1930, were said by Sir Frederick Kenyon, Director and Principal Librarian of the British Museum, to be proliferating like rabbits.

Several attempts have been made to use modern technology, particularly audiovisual aids, to produce instructional material illustrating these processes. Most of them are dreary enough to prevent anyone wanting ever to use a library, still less to master the intricacies of *Chemical abstracts* or the *British humanities index*. The reason for this lack of impact is not hard to find, and relates precisely to what I have been saying about presentation of information depending on the extent to which a particular viewpoint has human interest and the presenter strikes a chord in the imagination of the receiver.

Merely describing an excursion through the index and pages of a complex work of reference, such as *Chemical abstracts*, is highly unlikely to strike such a chord. As I have said, telling me the specific heat of mercury when I have no interest in mercury has no significance for me and will not arouse my interest unless it can be presented, not as a bald fact, but with such surrounding intellectual scenery that I can recognize how it fits my own state of mind. In one film designed to help University students in using local libraries, the scene is set in a library which is deserted save for a librarian fiddling about behind a desk, waiting to leap into action when the solitary user arrives with an enquiry. All the shelves are neat and tidy, and no sooner has the enquirer made known her problem than the librarian produces the necessary reference book, as if by magic, from a shelf by the desk. No part of this film is actually untrue, yet the total scene presented lacks all contact with reality as experienced by a library user. It may have convinced its producers of the value of a library to a new university student, but I doubt if the conviction lasted very long. Yet it can be done, as was shown by the entertaining and instructive film of the Library of Congress introduced on television by Sir Huw Wheldon.

Explanations of how to use a library, and how to use catalogues, indexes and other guides to specialist literature, all perform the same basic function, namely, to introduce the user to a means of access to the wealth of recorded information that now exists all over the world. Librarians have long been aware that, just as no subject exists in isolation, so no library, however large, can now hope to be self-sufficient in meeting all the needs of its actual and potential users. Kenyon himself pioneered schemes of inter-library cooperation in Britain, and for many years the National Central Library and the Regional Library Bureaux aspired to provide complete coverage of British publications in public libraries by means of subject specialization schemes based on the Decimal Classification and the *British national bibliography*.

A dramatic change in the philosophy of inter-library lending came with the founding of the National Lending Library for Science and Technology under the dynamic and pragmatic leadership of Donald Urquhart. His thesis, put simply, was that if the country provided one central store which contained all the scientific literature covered by indexes and abstracts, these could be used as the finding lists and enquirers would be able to go, via a local library, straight to the national centre, where they would be certain to find what they required. The outstanding success of this library, now with the National Central Library as the British Library Lending Division, testifies to the soundness of Urquhart's vision and the immense practical and political skill with which he put it into effect. Linked with the British Library Reference Division at the British Museum, and the existing network of regional co-operation, it could be said that any library in Britain provides an access point to collections from which virtually any enquiry can be answered.

The NCL had also acted as an agent for international interlending, and the BLLD has continued this to such great effect that some half a million of its three million or so annual loans go to countries overseas. Librarians and their users, especially in developing countries, have good reason for gratitude to Urquhart and the BLLD, and n libraries in the United States have said that they find it quicker to obtain material from BLLD than from each other.

The development of library services at the international level, though not new, has brought with it new problems for library practice; some of them, indeed, are old problems in new guises. The apparently safe ground of individual names, for example, became shifting sand and when international bibliographical standards brought in groups of Arabic, African, Chinese, Japanese and so forth. Although this was in practice an old problem for specialist libraries, as they were accustomed to Cyrillic and other non-Roman scripts, matters such as the correct spelling for William

Shakespeare had not exercised the minds of many librarians hitherto.

The International Federation of Library Associations, IFLA, encouraged by Unesco, accordingly began the programme of Universal Bibliographic Control, with an office in the British Library Reference Division run by an experienced librarian, Dorothy Anderson, who has published several accounts and progress reports. As she has pointed out, the possibilities for exploiting computers in the cataloguing of current publications stimulated the programme, but it had been discussed before, and several countries already had a national bibliographic service like the *British national bibliography*. Access for scholars to the world's output of publications could be greatly improved if each country were to record its own production in machine-readable form, and make it available either through a common data file, or, more likely, through a distributed network of compatible files.

The publishing world itself began to take seriously a similar prospect, that of simplifying the process of ordering books and journals. However standardized, names and titles can become long and complicated, and a very simple scheme of giving each document a unique number led to International Standard Book Numbers, ISBN, and International Standard Serial Numbers, ISSN. Each publisher has a set of numbers allocated by the national office, and the scheme has already proved its value in the saving of space on the computer file and in connect time when consulting it.

IFLA also organized two major conferences on cataloguing principles in 1961 and 1969, which aimed at providing standards for catalogues which could be accepted internationally – an essential element in universal bibliographic control. As a result, a series of International Standard Bibliographic Descriptions appeared between 1971 and 1980, covering all types of printed material, and some non-book material. These are the items which have produced the genuinely new problems, especially the analysis and standardization of the various elements in tapes, slides, floppy discs, hard discs, video discs, and all the other paraphenalia associated with the coming of records which are invisible to the naked eye and can only be consulted through a machine.

The other important component of a world service of access to current publishing followed more or less concurrently in the medium-term programme of IFLA and Unesco: Universal Availability of Publications. This grew naturally out of the great improvement in the availability of scientific works made by Urquhart at the NLLST and subsequently the BLLD; and most of the drive for UAP comes from Urquhart's successor as Director-General of BLLD, Maurice Line, who points out that 'there is little point in knowing that publications exist if they cannot be obtained when needed'. IFLA has an international advisory committee for UAP, and the Office for International Lending has been set up under Line's direction at the BLLD. Among the main activities of UAP are inter-library loan on the international level, reprography, systems of legal deposit and copyright, the use of computers for establishing inter-library networks, and improving the standards of national libraries.

With the help of Unesco, IFLA held an international Congress on UAP in Paris in May 1982. This was very well attended, and included publishers, booksellers, librarians, archivists, information specialists and government officials. The main sessions dealt with:
  – access and availability to users
  – production and supply of publications
  – acquisition policies and planning
  – repository policies and planning
  – national and international inter-lending policies and practices.

It might have been expected that the results of this conference would have been fresh in the minds of those taking part in organizing the World Congress on Books in the following month, but one looks in vain for any mention of it in the Congress *Final report*. Both meetings are, however, recalled in the recommendations of the World Conference on Cultural Policies in Mexico City. This does not appear under the heading of 'Culture, Information and Communication', which urges the Director-General of Unesco and Member States to push forward the International Programme for the Development of Communication, and is also very strong on the mass media and audiovisual materials. In the general section headed 'Production and Dissemination of Cultural Goods and Services —Culture Industries', Recommendation No 115, recalling Unesco's efforts to promote books and written media, and in particular the Congress on UAP and the World Congress on Books, recommends that Unesco:

(a) launch, within the limits of budgetary resources, and with the collaboration of the International Programme for the Development of Communication, an extensive programme for the world-wide promotion of books and written materials . . .
and

(b) collaborate, in the implementation of these activities, with other regional or inter-regional organizations for cultural co-operation, both governmental and non-governmental as well as foundations.

This Conference took a very wide view of the range of national culture as the basic element for progress and national development, and stressed the need for complementary policies in the fields of culture, education, science and communication in order to keep a harmonious balance between technological advances on the one hand, and intellectual and moral development on the other. Both are essential if nations are to grow in sympathy with one another. This makes it all the more urgent for those in authority to take part in national and international development on both fronts, and in my view the World Conference failed to acknowledge this. For although, in Recommendation No 60, it had regard to Unesco's activities in the field of information, 'in which use is made of modern libraries and archives', and asked Member

States to pay particular attention to them, this is in the context of 'Manuscripts, archives and documents'. One can only interpret this as putting the emphasis for libraries on their role as keepers, the traditional rather than the modern type of activity. Regretfully, the influence of the General Information Programme seems to be lacking.

Whether or not a strong contribution from the GIP would have laid stress on the role of libraries as finders and disseminators of information, we shall never know. What is clear, though, is that there is a need for information about what actually goes on in modern libraries to be given much wider currency, so that other organizers of the communication process, and those who make decisions about cultural and technical development will no longer remain under the illusion that libraries are only a part of history. The invention and refinement of techniques like author and subject catalogues, schemes of classification, reference and SDI services, show that librarians respond to new ways of recording and distributing information in society, and by professional action, both nationally and internationally, keep their organizations in step with, and sometimes in advance of, others who devote their efforts to the vital task of improving understanding among the people.

Chapter 6

TECHNOLOGY AND CULTURE

Perhaps the most important of all the principles and recommentations of the World Conference on Cultural Policies are those which emphasize the inevitable and inextricable interdependence of technology and culture. The history of mankind is a history of struggle to master and control the environment, and technology provides the means to do it. Science provides information about what could be done, technology about what can be done. All advance in scientific understanding, said Peter Medawar in his Romanes Lecture in 1968 'begins with a speculative adventure, an imaginative preconception of *what might be true* — a preconception which always, and necessarily, goes a little way (sometimes a long way) beyond anything which we have logical or factual authority to believe in'. Literature and art, the humanities, should provide us with insights into the human condition and how people are actually affected by progress in controlling the environment — and not forgetting that the environment includes communities of people.

The culture of a people represents the interaction of all these areas of human endeavour and adventure. It is the expression of an integrated society of whole, integrated people who know their world and cope with it by and through their relationships with each other. We need only look at the contemporary world to see how incomplete is our understanding of the environment.

The speculative adventure of the creative scientist, though

outstripping logical and factual authority, nevertheless begins with it. In Kuhn's paradigm theory, for example, in order to recognize a discrepancy, one has first of all to know what is the normal expectation. The essence of public knowledge is the consensus, the general agreement that such and such is the case, among the scholars and experts who know the details. A paradigm, a generally accepted picture of the real world at any epoch, rests on a secure foundation of tested facts and relationships, and this security is attained by the patient labour of those who accumulate the details and make them publicly available in records.

Libraries therefore provide access to the foundations for future advances, and a library which gives its users an active information service plays a crucial role in that it helps to set the scene for the next speculative adventure. Our knowledge of the environment, of the world out there and of each other, no longer depends on what we experience personally. The library service transcends the limitations of time and space, and by organizing its records for active use makes available the wisdom of the ages and the experience of today. As people become more aware of the nature of life and experience, their interest grows and should be nourished.

It is not enough for librarians merely to respond to new ways of recording and disseminating information. A more creative approach will come from a much greater involvement with both producers and consumers of information. What is required for this is an understanding of pattern, of the structure of relationships between Man and Nature and between Man and Man, nation and nation. This will not come from merely supplying masses of facts from the vastly increased output that characterizes the present age. Such an increase has long been known in science, and has indeed led to something of a crisis in science education: how to continue education in depth and still leave time for reflection and consideration to discover discrepancies and solve problems by original research. Now, the situation has been exacerbated by radio and television, bringing their continuous supply of instant information from all over the world. Even newspapers are no longer instant enough for the appetite that the media are creating, and constantly face crises and uncertainties about their future. But when instant information is closely followed by instant obliteration, the chances of building a foundation for cultural progress begin to disappear.

The crisis over the 'two cultures' illustrates how a dangerous rift may develop between science and the humanities because of over-specialization on both sides and the failure to nourish the general view of culture exemplified by the early history of the Royal Society. The state of the scientific literature shows how much the scientific research process has changed since Darwin took more than twenty years to convince himself that he had enough information to justify publishing *The origin of species*; even then, the final spur was applied by Wallace. Nowadays, such are the mountains of facts publicly available in every corner of every field, most research has become a matter of teamwork in institutions. These programmes have become independent of individuals, and the teams are but elements in a continuous process, who have to make their presence known by publishing, not the record of completed projects, but every step, no matter how trivial, along a never-ending road. The scientific literature has become choked with information of no particular significance for anyone but the authors themselves. Kuhn goes so far as to suggest that the scientist who takes the trouble to write a whole book may well find that his professional reputation has been damaged rather than enhanced.

This does not quite cover the case; Kuhn's own book makes an exception, like that of Ziman. Peter Medawar, W I B Beveridge, Jacob Bronowski, are among quite a large number of eminent scientists who have not only written books, but chosen to collect together some of their previously published articles or television lectures, precisely in order to give them greater permanence. One of the greatest furores of this century was provoked by the publication of J D Watson's *The double helix* in 1968.

But in general, in what Kuhn called 'normal science', the significance of the single author has declined, and the subject approach to the literature has almost replaced the search on authors' names. The literature reflects this by the large numbers of articles with '*et al.*' type of authorship. Even the innovative *Citation indexes* of Eugene Garfield's Institute for Scientific Information usually require an entry through a subject. The function of these indexes is to trace the influence of authors on the development of their subject by linking their own papers with those of other authors who cite them, but the author sequences are supplemented by sophisticated *Permuterm indexes* without which it would be extremely difficult to start many a search.

In the face of this enormous outpouring of subject information, now often, and often wrongly, called 'data', information technology appears to offer a brilliant answer to the question of how to control it and make it available. One of the crasser results of this is the tendency to downgrade libraries and to predict that books and libraries will eventually disappear; even some librarians have written large and superficial books heralding the approach of the paperless society.

Among the prophets of the new age, one of the most conspicuous was Marshall McLuhan, whose concept of the 'global village' ought to inspire us to work towards the achievement of all that the term connotes. For obviously this is not limited to the mere statement, nor even of an extended definition. The real attraction lies in the whole picture summoned up by the imagination of all the concepts we have learned to associate with the idea of a village: small distances, convenient access to services, easy coping with daily life, above all the sense of knowing people in a community, of neighbourliness based on continuous, more or less permanent human relationships. Yet McLuhan's most famous book contradicts all this, by its very title, *The medium is the message*. Not 'carries' the message, but 'is'. The reality of this is that there is no message, no content, only form. It can only lead to cultural decline, because form, especially technological form, has no human significance of its own, and therefore no permanence. It cannot, of itself alone, make any contribution to the cultural heritage.

Of course, the advocates of the paperless society do not see things quite like this. They see the need for improved communication, to be sure; but they interpret communication in the narrow sense of 'information transfer', of moving 'bits' from here to there. They look forward to a society in which all knowledge is reduced to information stored in computer files with access to it readily available by on-line consultation at a terminal. Even where this question-and-answer way of life does not encompass every human need, the terminal still suffices because it also provides references to articles in journals which in turn are only available on-line. A few odd and doubtless insignificant people may still want to read books, or do what is contemptuously dismissed as 'literary research', and this may in extreme cases require a visit to such libraries as may still exist for the sake of their 'archives'.

Such a view, now propagated by many who may be presumed to have the well-being of the people at heart, is to my mind superficial and indeed dangerous to the health of the international community, and this makes it all the more necessary to cast grave suspicion on the World Conference Report's placing of libraries only in the context of manuscripts and archives. It is all the more surprising, when one reflects that the first Minister for Information Technology in Britain has a reputation as a poet.

McLuhan himself provides the key to the puzzle. If the medium is indeed the message, and if the improvement of communication is the objective, it follows that research and development must concentrate on the medium, which is not only the means of communication, but also its end.

Once the user has typed his question into the terminal, and up comes 'the answer', that is supposedly the end of the matter until the next question comes along.

Every professional librarian knows that a certain amount of library use does indeed come into this class; many enquiries are of the 'specific heat of mercury' type, and many enquirers are looking for lists of references which can easily and speedily be supplied on-line from a public data base of which there are now hundreds. On-line access to many bits of information will certainly improve the lives of many people. We have every incentive to encourage computer manufacturers to go on improving their machines and their software to fit the situations we meet in libraries, and it is the case that some of these manufacturers have begun to realize that information transfer, in the library sense, means more than what is very appropriately named number-crunching.

Among his 'Five Laws of Library Science' Ranganathan included as the fourth law, 'Save the time of the reader', and on-line retrieval of information from large, or specialized, data bases, does just that. Looking through annual volumes of indexes and abstracts in pursuit of relevant books and articles can be a tedious and time-consuming business. Even the cumulative indexes of essential tools like the *British national bibliography* and *Chemical abstracts* are expensive to buy and ponderous to use. Many publishers appreciate the great advantage offered by on-line consultation and are building up retrospective files so that many more years of their publications can be consulted at one sitting. In the University of London alone, over 5,000 such searches were made in 1982. Before many years are past, library catalogues will all be converted into machine-readable form; already organizations like the many co-operative groups in Britain and the United States share their records of current acquisitions.

No one doubts that new technology already has, among its many abilities, the power to convert, more or less cheaply, the catalogues of even the largest libraries and to provide access to them simply through the public telephone system. The reason why this is not being done rapidly and systematically does not lie in any shortcomings of the technology. It lies in other causes, partly due to the reluctance of librarians to undertake what looks like a large operation, partly due to the fierce competition between computer makers who are busily producing new models every week and taking good care to ensure that there is little compatibility among them. As with information transfer itself, the problems that remain unsolved are social, and not technical, problems. Even the wasteful proliferation of new machines depends on a market — enough people being persuaded that the new machines would be good for them.

On the management side, that is, the organization of institutions carrying out certain regulating processes, often known as 'housekeeping', nearly all their operations offer some scope for mechanization. If we regard the total institution as consisting of stock, readers and services, a brief look at each of these readily shows how far in fact automation has already progressed.

From the housekeeping point of view, 'stock' resolves itself into the collection of items and making them available as particular objects — getting them on the shelves and establishing systems for lending and reference. On entry into the system of publication a record is created for a book in a publisher's list; a periodical article appears on a list of contents of a particular issue of a particular journal. National and international standards are already available for such descriptions, while quick reference can be made via ISBN and ISSN. The 'books on order' file of a library again records the details of items required; these details may themselves have been copied from reviews in newspapers or reading lists distributed by lecturers. When a book arrives, it begins its travels through accession numbering, cataloguing, classification, labelling of one sort and another, until it comes to rest, temporarily, in the place where potential readers will find it. Any item of stock which has a separate independent existence as an object will go through more or less the same processes.

A periodical article will not usually have such an existence, but be bound up with several others, so that the actual processing may be somewhat different, though the objective and the general principle are the same. The point is that the same information is being recorded over and over again, when common sense would seem to indicate that once was enough. Experience already shows that the creation of an entry in a computerized file at the point of ordering will do this, provided that all those who may have to consult the record have easy access to a terminal. There are no technical problems involved in adding or amending entries on-line, so that classification symbols and similar location marks, and the marks of identity of separate copies of the same book, can easily be added. A system such as this ought to eliminate the backlogs of books which have arrived but are so far not catalogued, which cause anxious moments to many conscientious librarians.

Similarly, the sharing of records relating to individuals, whether staff or readers, presents no technical problems. A public library may well have access to records created by other departments of the local authority, and a university library should be able to share the records created by the registrar. Some social considerations may intervene: care must be taken that only information relevant to the library's requirements are borrowed, and the wise librarian will take care to consult trade unions or students' associations in order to ensure remaining within the bounds of personal privacy.

Librarians are no longer strangers to the opportunities offered by computers in the processing of records involved in the management of libraries. The consideration of readers brings us back to the question of services. What does a library offer its readers, and how far does the prospect of a paperless society actually affect them? It will not matter how efficiently the housekeeping activities are automated if the sort of library services for which they provide are made obsolete by the progress of the same technology.

I believe that we are being badly misled by a confusion between ends and means. Information technology is a means, a method of carrying out a set of processes, just as the book catalogue and the card catalogue were, in their time, means and methods derived from existing technology. The various forms of microdocuments are means to solve problems arising from shortage of space, but as library records, particularly as catalogues on microfiche, they are likely to have only a temporary use, and be superseded by the on-line file. The earliest applications of computers in libraries often turned out to be disastrous, because the people involved had not analysed the differences between information transfer and number-crunching. The aim of using electronic devices, of any kind, in libraries is similar to the aim of using them in newspaper offices, which is to improve the efficiency of routine processes. If the mere process of information transfer itself becomes accepted as the end, and not only the means, then we should be eminently justified in seeking more, and more powerful, machines in order to raise our productivity and transfer ever increasing numbers of bits.

Looked at in this light, the extinction of the library as an institution of society (except for 'archives') need arouse no pangs of remorse in the minds of anyone, least of all of librarians themselves. No one regrets the replacement of the pen by the typewriter for making catalogue cards. It was a more efficient way of doing the same thing, giving access to the stock – the books, periodicals, etc – and it was taken for granted that access was, for the reader, only the beginning of the process of information transfer. Books and periodicals, as library stock, had been in use for centuries and were believed to have performed a useful social function.

What the paperless society envisages, however, is not the

replacement of the typewriter alone, but the replacement also of the book and periodical. The guide to the records has become one with the records themselves. So we are no longer speaking about the use of automation in libraries but about the use of automation instead of libraries, the medium as the message. This involves not only libraries, but the whole practice of publication of documents and their use by readers.

Such a prospect cannot be accepted by anyone who believes in the existence of a cultural heritage and looks to new technology to improve it. I cannot seriously imagine that the writers of large books prophesying the paperless society actually believe in the prospect that their work, and the considered and sometimes profound thought which it embodies, will in the not-too-distant future be reduced to a row of bits to be read on a television screen. Perhaps they regard themselves as being part of the 'archives'? Or perhaps as lecturers reciting what would otherwise have been published as books?

Most of the time, the future looks like being a combination of the tried and tested, and the new and interesting. The reality of the present situation is that, as far as libraries are concerned, books and periodicals are more used by more people than ever before; in the most modern libraries, this is precisely because access to relevant information has been greatly improved by means of automated guides to the sources. Even for the most instant information, the radio and television news services, the most successful information transfer occurs when the statement of what is happening by a talking head is elaborated by showing the actual scene, or by a blow-by-blow account from the man on the spot. Television series which genuinely aim at enhancing human experience, such as Kenneth Clark on 'Civilization', Jacob Bronowski on 'The ascent of Man', Alistair Cooke on 'America', immediately reappear as books.

A moment's thought shows why. It is simply because their authors, and the television authorities, believe that such works have more to give than the temporary impact of the instant viewing. They believe that these works have some permanent value for humanity and that the book is the proper way to preserve it. A good book, as Milton said, is 'the precious life blood of a master spirit, embalmed and treasured up on purpose to a life beyond life', and, we may add, a good library is the means by which that purpose is fulfilled. This cannot be so unless the recipient of information has time to reflect, and consider how this may be assimilated into his present store. He has to pause and make a considered judgement.

The fact is that behind some paperless society writings one can detect the baleful influence of behaviourist psychology and the philosophy of pragmatism. Since most of it comes from the United States, where these two influences have sunk most deeply into the national consciousness, this is not surprising; but it is alarming.

For the questions that are not asked in these writings are the most important of all: who is the information for, and what will they do with it when they have it? Let us also remember that the idea of the paperless society is not new. It was, in fact, invented long before the electronic computer, in 1932, when Aldous Huxley published *Brave new world*. When all members of society are machine-conditioned to accept a way of life not far removed from bread and circuses, all individual freedom disappears and the cultural heritage becomes extinct. The eminent and influential biologist, Paul Weiss, has emphasized the human need for challenge and incentive, because an effortless existence becomes a tranquillizing drug.

Challenge and incentive certainly come from direct experience of life, but unless we are to revert to the state of a primitive society based only on man-machine interaction, the challenges to our minds will continue to come mainly from opportunities to consider and reflect at leisure on those ideas of others which they think have sufficient value to be preserved in libraries.

There is grave danger for humanity in the prospect of everyone sitting at home in front of television terminals and imagining that they have access to all information (except, of course, the literary researchers with their archives). The danger lies in the isolation from any community of individuals who share information, in the widest sense, and the consequent trivialization of what is presented on the screen, because it takes more than passive reception to arouse the sense of real human significance. The spectacle of men walking on the Moon, of itself, was far less exciting than any episode of a well-made science fiction film. What transformed it from a primitive example of such a film into 'a giant step for mankind' was that it represented the culmination of a great and heroic adventure – or rather a series of adventures that began, not in the United States, but in the USSR, when a little sphere called Sputnik went around the world in space and returned safely to earth.

Now it has been suggested, though not seriously, that the Moon walk was indeed a science fiction film, and the fact is that it could have been. All the technology to make such film is readily available, and we know already that Nature (including people) imitates Art (incuding science fiction). What I find alarming are the implications of rows of people sitting by a bank of computer terminals controlling the destinies of others, the astronauts, to whom they are linked only by the sound of disembodied voices. All direct human contact has gone. Great events are directed simply by pressing buttons.

If this basic human process of communication ends up as a matter of pressing buttons at a computer terminal, technology has become totally isolated from culture, and has become an end in itself. Librarians, in their traditional role as keepers of the records, ought to regard this as a challenge to traditional practices, and an incentive to change them. So far, information services have developed mainly in special libraries serving science and industry. Most other libraries have made use of modern technology, but efforts to break out of the traditional roles have not so far become standard practice. Surely, an opportunity occurs here which it would be folly to ignore.

National, university and public libraries are the main stores of traditional information, the cultural heritage. Special libraries in industry do not, as a rule, supply multiple copies of textbooks or recreational fiction and literature. They do provide an active service of information supply to their colleagues, and this plays an essential part in enabling research workers both to solve technical problems and to devise new technologies. In brief, librarians in special libraries have become information officers who are more concerned with communicating messages than with elaborating media. This is not to confuse information science with information theory. Information theory sprang from the science of telecommunications, and concerns itself with the flow of information as the movement of electrons; in other words, with the efficiency of the medium. It does not concern itself with the meaning of the information transferred, any more than the parrot which says 'Good morning' at any hour of the day or night.

The way in which librarians can take part in the task of bridging the gaps between technology and culture, now more socially necessary than ever before, is to bring the dynamism of information service into the areas of the social sciences and humanities. This means a closer association with all who are engaged in the process of communication, exemplified by the individuals and organizations present at the two Unesco Conferences, and those participating in the International Programme for the Development of Communication. It means to bring the traditional 'bibliographical' expertise into play with the techniques of information services, in order to help advance culture, as information officers help to advance science and technology.

This means enlarging, rather than changing, the role of the librarian, as some would maintain. Introducing the techniques of automation has already begun to free librarians from routines like cataloguing which were, in the past, considered an essential ingredient of scholarship, as scholarship was an essential ingredient of cataloguing. It still is, for some classes of material, and still requires expert study. But the sharing of records and access made possible by computers frees librarians from much routine that has become mere drudgery, and makes them available for information services in all types of library, and in all fields of knowledge.

The tensions and discrepancies that build up and finally cause dramatic changes in our view of the world are evident in library and information science as in many other areas of human endeavour. By virtue of the very range of library materials available for exploitation, librarians now have this opportunity to widen their own horizons, to come out into society, so to speak, and add their own characteristic effort to improve communication. There is a great need for all engaged in this to recognize the contributions of each other, in order that harmonious collaboration may assist bewildered humanity to struggle through to a more mature civilization. As Lord Adrian said in his presidential address to the British Association for the Advancement of Science many years ago, 'the control which has been achieved by science has made it possible for us to improve our own natures by more education in the arts of civilized life'.

At such an historic moment, when new technology offers librarians and information officers the chance to make a real contribution to enhancing the cultural heritage by active exploitation of all its records, it would be a tragic irony if the medium became the message, technology became the master and not the servant, and librarians found themselves once more cast in the role of keepers, not of books, but of machines. This would scarcely contribute to the advancement of learning through merchants of light, but resemble rather the proposals for a philosophical college put forward by Abraham Cowley in 1661, whose company included 'a Library-keeper, who is likewise to be Apothecary, Druggist, and Keeper of Instruments, Engines, etc'.

Chapter 7

THEORY AND PRACTICE

The headlong progress of computer technology over recent decades has carried along all those of us engaged in communication at an exhilarating pace. Learned societies, publishers, librarians, have all become convinced of the necessity of making publicly available every last thought, no matter how commonplace or trivial, so that it may be indexed, abstracted, put into machine-readable form, and displayed on a visual display unit.

The benefits of the new technology are indeed not to be denied, and it would be foolish to try to keep it out of libraries. But if technology is not to become the master, then library and information science requires an advance in its theoretical foundations, and this must play an important part in the preparation of future members of the profession.

It must be clear by now that when speaking of 'the profession', I do not subscribe to the view that information transfer, as an active service, is beyond the scope of librarians, who are presumed to be locked in their traditional function of keeping the books (and no doubt the engines, etc). On the contrary, I believe in the unity of a profession which includes librarians of all kinds of library, and information specialists, who may very well represent the advance guard in these times, but should not lose contact with the main body. If some libraries are required to function as archives, and in doing so fulfil a necessary social function, it does not follow that all others should do the same. If this were so, there might well be a case for condemning them to extinction, as Jesse Shera used to say, like the whaling industry of Nantucket.

For the moment, there seems to be no single word to embrace what I understand by 'library and information service', and I tend to use 'library' as a generic term. Unesco uses 'information' in its NATIS concept, the idea of the national information service which includes the infrastructure of a network of libraries. But I hope and believe that a cross-fertilization of ideas is now taking place between the ancient art of librarianship, the activities of information scientists, the computer specialists, the arts of the new communications media, together with influences from basic sciences such as psychology and linguistics.

Much of the professional scholarship of librarians has been based on the study of the book as a physical object, its cataloguing and enumeration in lists on various subjects. Bibliography, analytical and subject, will no doubt continue to form part of professional study, and should, because it forms a link between those professions involved in the production side of the communications network, the publishers and booksellers. Subject bibliography plays its part at the use end of the spectrum of professional activities in linking librarians with subject specialists and research workers.

Knowledge of books, and care of the book as a physical object, its textual history, various editions, and bibliographical description, have a continuing role to perform among the arts of civilized life.

Information officers have historically based their claim to be a separate profession on the possession of subject knowledge rather than on efficiency and scholarship in the handling of objects, however rare, beautiful or venerable. In practice, this claim often turned out to rest on knowledge of source materials in subjects, as was shown by the alacrity with which scientific information officers extended their range in order to include the newly developing activities in industry of economic information systems and market research. In practice, one can detect no real difference between this kind of knowledge of source materials from that which any librarian rapidly acquires from reference service by personal contact with readers and learning which sources provide the most useful information.

When first suggesting the term 'Informatics' to mean a unified concept embracing a range of disciplines, including information services in the social sciences and humanities, A I Mikhailov and R S Giljarevskij placed this new discipline in the context of the social sciences, and claimed that it is 'in a way a continuation of bibliography and library service, but the experience inherited by informatics from these branches of science is being subjected to a complete reappraisal and appears in a new quality'. The original curriculum for the new discipline was as follows:

> Informatics and laws of sciences (ie knowledge) development
> Interrelation of Informatics with other fields of knowledge
> General concept of information
> Theory of information retrieval systems
> Linguistics problems of Informatics
> Information languages and classification problems
> Psychological problems of Informatics
> Study of information needs and inquiries
> Efficiency of scientific information activity, its criteria and indices
> Theoretical basis for reasonable presentation of scientific information
> The role of hardware in science information activity.

'Science' in this table is used in the general European sense of *scientia* or *Wissenschaft*, meaning the whole of knowledge and not only the physical and natural sciences. Their later *Guide for an introductory course* laid more stress on the traditional side of librarianship, but still emphasized the need to include several areas of theoretical study hitherto considered to be outside the scope of professional education.

In marking out an area for the theoretical foundation of library and information services in the general field of communications, I am fully in accord with Patrick Williams and Joan Thornton Pearce when they claim, in their valuable and significantly titled essay, *The vital network*, that 'Communication professionals need a theoretical model. Technical expertise alone is not sufficient. In addition to expertise, a professional needs a philosophical understanding of his activity and of its importance to human beings and to society'. The last part of their book contains a veiled attack on the American communications industry and the way in which the search for bigger and bigger production works towards the degradation rather than the enhancement of the quality of life.

The object of a model should be to define the limits of operation in general terms, as a system which has an internal unity and integrity, but which also manifests points of access with the surrounding countryside, so that practitioners in librarianship become fully aware of their own relations with the adjacent professions, while they in turn can see where common interests develop and should work in harmony. Working along the lines of the three major aspects of the communication flow, the following outline seems to me to provide a model and the appropriate links or points of access to related disciplines:

— The universe of knowledge

   Study of the nature, forms and disciplines of knowledge, the inner structure of subject information, and the external relations between subjects.

— Production and publication of information

   The processes of research, discovery and communication; formal and informal systems of communication, publishing, the news media. Role of the book trade. Primary and secondary documents. Reprography.

— Acquisition and arrangement of materials

   Bibliography: information about documents, and their

sources. Classification and cataloguing. Structure of indexing languages and retrieval systems.
— Dissemination and use of information
Methods of distribution, current awareness service. Psychology of users, sociology of user groups and their need for information.
— Library and information service technology
Use (not manufacture) of all types of equipment, audio-visuals, computers. Basic introduction to their intellectual foundations, 'expert systems' and artificial intelligence.
— Planning and management of libraries
— Comparative and historical studies
Study of national and international systems and organizations. Comparative analysis as scientific method applied to each area of the model.

This may at first blush appear to range far more widely than what one might expect, but many supporting studies already exist, like those of Belkin, Kemp, McGarry, and the monumental and highly popular *Subject approach to information* of Foskett (A C).

I am dealing here with a theoretical model, of course, and the nature of any particular course of professional education will naturally depend on the specializations of teachers and the ambitions of students in their selection of options from such a wide range of offerings. Every institution of advanced or professional study has to face up to the relationship between theory and practice; it has always been a fruitful source of argument, and doubtless will continue to be so. In my view, excellence in practical skills can only be acquired in a real-life situation, but there must be an element of practical work in a course devoted to professional theory because theory without practice is sterile. Practice without theory is blind, however, and the better the theoretical grasp, the firmer and more effective the practical experience.

The task of a professional course of education is to provide for the student an initiation into a body of accepted theory and practice, by means of which he will be able, not only to deal with the actual situations which arise in the course of his work, but also to formulate for himself the role he feels called upon to play, his duties and responsibilities, in the light of a professional consensus. By means of a sound grasp of theory, he will also be able to discern where an evolving practice, responding to developing social needs, has rendered the same theory outmoded and ripe for change. What characterizes a *science*, as distinct from a technology, is that it consists of a body of information, commonly accepted as true, generalized by abstraction from a body of experience and observation of individual phenomena. Such a body of information cannot claim to be a science if it consists only of a series of descriptions unrelated to one another and so existing in isolation, like peas in a bag. 'Why do we believe in scientific knowledge?' asks John Ziman, and answers 'The strongest argument, surely, is that a theory provides a logical ordering, a pattern, for observations'.

Through the study of 'the universe of knowledge', of systems of classification and indexing languages, the librarian acquires a general picture of this logical order and pattern in art and literature as well as in science, and should be able to relate his own pattern of thought and his knowledge of sources to what a user may already know when he comes to make a request for more information. This is the basic situation, though there may, and often do, arise other more elaborate or complicated meeting of minds between librarians and users.

One thing is certain: information service from a library must be tailored to fit the actual needs of actual users. There is no point in piling more and bigger computer-produced bibliographical masterpieces on the laps or desks of people who seek help precisely because they are weighed down with the mass of information they already have, and cannot see the pattern for the multiplicity of threads. Unless what is provided has real meaning, the recipient will regard it as another burden rather than a blessed relief. Information has meaning in two main ways: it may relate to the existing state of knowledge in a subject, the paradigm; it may relate to the context of thought already existing in the user's mind, that is, the picture he has of the subject he is interested in, and his uncomfortable feeling that what he has is what Belkin calls an 'anomalous state of knowledge'.

Several attempts have been made to clarify what we mean when we say that certain information is 'relevant' to a particular discussion. In some polemics, one side often accuses the other of introducing 'irrelevant' material, by which is usually meant information which may relate to the subject under discussion but which they do not wish to admit. In Information Theory, the word 'noise' is used to mean information which does not appear to clarify a message, and is therefore superfluous, an interference with efficient transmission of the precise terms of the message.

In order to make a clear distinction between the two main meanings of information in this context of users' needs, I believe that a sound solution is to use 'relevance' and 'pertinence'. This was done regularly some years ago in discussions on measuring the effectiveness of information services when C W Cleverdon, in the classic series of tests known as the Aslib/Cranfield experiment, first introduced the concepts of Recall and Precision. Recall, the mathematical measure of that proportion of library stock produced by one set of index terms, relates to subject specification: Precision, the measure of that proportion which satisfies an enquiry, relates to user specification. Cleverdon's work suggested that, generally speaking, the higher the Recall, the lower the Precision, and while subsequent research indicates the need to refine the theory, practical experience shows that it does indeed provide a useful guide in making a literature search, including searching on a computer file, where high Recall can be very expensive and lead to an increase in the amount of 'noise'.

Relevance and Pertinence, as distinguishable concepts, relate in a similar way to the context of thought in a user's mind. A typical request, expressed in apparently precise terms, might be 'the influence of A in the use of B in the process C to produce D', where A, B, C, and D are terms used in the index language or subject catalogue of the library stock. A search in the index using these terms leads to a document dealing exactly with the subject as specified. This is clearly relevant, because it relates exactly to the existing state of knowledge in that subject, and there is no disagreement between the user and the result of the search. But he has already read this document, and does not wish to see it again. Is it pertinent to his request? Equally clearly it is not. But the library system, its index language, has not failed to supply material relevant to the subject as specified. Suppose, as an alternative hypothesis, that the user has not in fact seen this document before, but on reading it he finds that it makes no contribution to his own stock of knowledge because it gives him no information that he did not have already. Again, the system for retrieving material relevant to the subject specified has not failed, but the document retrieved has no pertinence to this particular request. On another occasion, it might have a high pertinence for a different user who puts his request in precisely the same form.

The difficulty in applying this entirely practical test as a mathematical measure of efficiency, as in a cost-benefit analysis, is that it is impossible to quantify in terms of the retrieval ability of a system, because the user will not be able to assess the value of any document until he has had the opportunity to examine it. He may also make a different assessment of the same document on two different occasions.

Relevance, therefore, means being part of the paradigm, or public knowledge, or consensus, the body of publicity available and accepted information which describes and defines a particular subject field; pertinence means being seen to be related to the specific context of thought in a particular user's mind, which may in turn be liable to change, and may not necessarily coincide with the consensus. An information service can at times become itself a stimulus to creativity by providing a user with what is pertinent even though it may seem irrelevant. Chance favours the prepared mind, and such serendipitous information is often the sort that leads to scientific revolutions.

Success in the process of Recall depends on having access to a collection of documents. Access has been greatly improved by increases in library resources and in the extent to which new technology has made possible the sharing of access to records, whether union catalogues of groups of libraries or public data bases like those provided by the Lockheed and Systems Development Corporations in the United States, and the Euronet Diane System in Western Europe. IFLA's projects for Universal Bibliographic Control and Universal Availability of Publications are practical implementations of the theoretical principle that no library, even the largest, can set out to supply all the potential needs of its body of users.

Accepting all this, it remains true that the convenience of the user will best be served, and his time saved, if what he wants is in fact available on the spot, at the library he is using. The day of the librarian as purely a collector is past, and it is a misuse of librarianship theory to persist in the 'we have everything' approach. This does not at all mean that the librarian need no longer have a theory to guide his collecting activities. On the contrary, in setting out to provide an information service related to users' needs, in this age of massive quantities of publications, the theory of selection stands more than ever in need of refinement. The opportunities for sharing collections envisaged by the UAP programme should not be allowed to lead to carelessness in selection, an abandoning of the traditional and still basic responsibility of building a collection that goes as far as possible towards meeting the immediate needs of the community of users, whether it be in a city, a university, or the research department of an industrial firm. Speed of supply in such a firm may be crucial in solving a technical problem in a factory or gaining a trading advantage over a competitor.

The 'good collection' nowadays means the collection that has been selected to make the best use of limited resources, in the context of national and international systems of co-operation, in meeting the needs of users by providing the most convenient form of access to actual documents as well as to factual information and references shown on a VDU.

To illustrate the practical effects of this approach, we may look at some of the ways in which selection policies in university libraries have developed. Panizzi's theory for the British Museum Library in the nineteenth century had considerable influence: in the world of rare books and specialist collections, for example, a university librarian could congratulate himself if he was able to secure everything that chanced to come his way, whether or not it bore any relation to the current teaching and research programmes. Some librarians now have cause to regret this enthusiasm, when they find valuable space occupied by large folio editions of standard authors which have long been superseded.

The primary duty of a university library is to provide the most convenient access to all the documents that relate to teaching and research. In acquiring and preserving the records of scholarship, a university library could reasonably claim to represent the personality of its university, and indeed the University Grants Committee described it as 'the central organ' in its first annual report in 1921. Every university teacher ensures that his subject is well represented in the library, so that the stock in each subject illustrates its development, over centuries in some libraries. Since the collection consists of works used in the teaching and research, and every teacher likewise ensures that his own publications are there, the library also illustrates the contribution that its university has made to the advancement of learning.

But the librarians of universities make their own contribution, because they occupy a privileged position. They see the collection as an integrated whole, representing the entire cultural heritage, and not as a series of separate subjects. They have a duty to the cultural heritage, in making sure that the students have the opportunity to see it as an integrated whole, even though the main preoccupation of each student may be to pass examinations by concentrating on reading lists issued by tutors. By collecting also those works which may not be on any such list, but which have won public esteem, librarians help to demonstrate the interrelatedness of all fields of knowledge. The professional techniques of cataloguing and classification are designed to achieve this end. Without the librarian's overview, the library would hardly come together as a whole, reflecting the wholeness of the universe of knowledge itself; it would remain a number of separate sections, and each teacher would be encouraged to persist in the unwelcome habit of referring to 'my section'. Some sections would doubtless receive more attention than others and distort the general picture.

As the heart of the university, the library inspires the affection of its readers, and their gratitude often finds expression in the prefaces to theses and books. Gifts ranging from single books, the precious life-blood of the authors, to large and splendid collections, testify to the respect in which these libraries are held, and to the belief of the donors in the lasting value of their gifts.

Although in a rather more specialized way, special and public libraries have a similar role to play in their own communities. The research department of an industrial firm will certainly wish to have in its library copies of all the scientific and other publications of the firm's members, such as market surveys, technical instruction manuals, and especially patents. As with university scientists, collections of laboratory notebooks and reports have lasting personal value, and it is by no means exceptional to find ideas discarded years ago being revised and succeeding in new circumstances, such as the invention of new equipment.

Many public libraries contain the best-known collections of the works of local authors; perhaps the most famous of all is the Shakespeare collection at Birmingham City Library. But a local collection graces nearly all public libraries, and is recognized as the major source for the history and culture of the town and its neighbourhood. The use of such collections is not confined to those interested in history and literature. Very often the local collection contains the only remaining copies of documents relating to the architecture, the commerce, engineering works such as the sites of drains and sewers, markets and highways, property boundaries.

Building a collection in the light of concepts of relevance and pertinence adds a new and searching focus to the process of selecting material for the stock. The library has its own personality, which determines the general nature of its contribution to the community, and it is from this source that positive action in improving communication through information service. Lately, for example, public libraries in Britain and the United States have very actively promoted 'outreach' programmes to bring to socially disadvantaged groups valuable information which they did not even know existed.

Unless the selection process is founded on such relationships and on an educated perception, on the part of librarians, of their role in the modern communications world, there is a danger that enthusiasm for the great possibilities in new technology may lead to the opposite of the desired objectives. So far from bringing in the paperless society, computers are producing more paper than ever before; much of its is utterly ephemeral, and some of it is utter rubbish. We should not allow the gods of increased production to fool us into believing that libraries must collect everything simply because it is published. John Kenneth Galbraith warned us, in *The affluent society* that 'The engines of mass communication in their highest state of development, assail the eyes and ears of the community on behalf of more beer but not of more schools'.

Libraries should no longer be looked upon as ready-made markets for everything that may somehow get published. There is nothing to be gained from processing vast quantities of information merely to show what vast quantities we can process. Librarians and libraries must be seen to take a positive part in the development of communication, based on professional judgement of the value of documents in promoting understanding because, in the words of the Unesco General Conference of 1966, 'each culture has a dignity and value which must be respected and preserved, and every people has the right and duty to develop its culture'.

Chapter 8

MEMORY AND ANTICIPATION

In organizing collections for information service, in relation to the communication process, pride of place goes to the two functions of retrospective searching and current awareness. These require a sound organizational foundation, to be sure; the management of libraries has reached the degree of sophistication and complexity characteristic of government ministries and large corporations. Many large books have been written on these aspects, and it is not my intention to add to them, but this certainly does not mean that I underrate their importance in providing the foundation.

We are engaged all our lives in learning about the world we live in, and the incentive to increase our own store of information arises directly from our wish, and our need, to form rational ideas, an ordered and consistent system of concepts. We examine instances and phenomena, observe the systems of relationships which they exhibit, and increase our understanding of bringing this information into association with what we know already, what is already stored in our memory. We do not simply add more and more separate items of information and leave them lying around in disordered heaps. If we did not attempt to give structure to our thoughts, there would be no way to relate new experience to old, or improve our control over our environment. We should never know what to expect from our experience of life from day to day.

Our whole understanding of the world is based on this

kind of expectation, that there is an order in nature, and that we can come to understand it, and to form a good idea of how events are likely to develop. We can, in a word, predict. We can land men on the Moon because we have predicted from our observations where it will be when they have travelled far enough to reach it. We do not simply aim a rocket at the Moon where we can see it, like a marksman at a target.

Memory plays an essential part in this, and in the whole of the learning process, and it is impossible to overestimate the value of order and structure in one's store of concepts. The eminent American educationist, Jerome S Bruner, often stressed the point that the discovery of the relations of similarity and difference is fundamental to the development of an educated person, and that it is necessary to understand these fundamentals and not only to take note of instances: 'Perhaps the most basic thing that can be said about human memory, after a century of intensive research, is that unless detail is placed into a structured pattern, it is rapidly forgotten'.

When we search our memory, it is because our mind has received a new stimulus and begins a search for related stimuli which we received previously and stored in a coherent structure. In Vygotsky's terms, we converted our 'spontaneous concepts' received from sensory perceptions into 'scientific concepts' which we can use to advance our understanding. In materialist terms, we create a system of circuitry so that a stimulus applied to one point will activate a linkage to other points in the circuit, calling to mind the nodes and the links in order to re-create a whole pattern which will be able to incorporate new nodes, new items of information.

It was not for nothing that Ranganathan called a library an externalized memory. With the enormous growth in education, research and the publication of information, no one today could make the claim attributed, even if mythically, to Benjamin Jowett that 'there is no knowledge but I know it'.

We all need, at some time or another, to have reference to information records to supplement our own memory. A collection of documents in systematic order has more reference points than a single mind, and library catalogues and classification schemes must therefore give access to a larger collection of information than could be managed by a single user. It must represent the cultural heritage, insofar as a selection can be made which conveniently reflects the interests of any particular community of users, so that any member of the community can call on the resources in an area of interest in order to complement and enlarge the information he already has.

Library catalogues and classification schemes provide the keys to these resources, and should therefore reflect the associations and links between ideas as they have already been described and explained by authors contributing to the publicly available store. The multiplicity of channels through which a user may travel to reach items of information is nicely illustrated by B C Vickery in his acute analysis of the nature of information science, based on long experience in industry, in national and academic libraries, and as a university teacher in this subject (see figure opposite).

Library classification has to put into systematic order the literature that is actually written, that is, the writer's understanding of reality; it deals with real things and the real relations that exist between them, but their presentation in any one document is necessarily influenced by being related also to the particular pattern of thought existing in the writer's mind. Many barriers may exist between the reality that is experienced and described by a writer, and the understanding of that reality comprehended by a reader; but the closer the description approximates to the reality, the more effective it is likely to be in organizing the thoughts of a reader who already has a partial understanding.

A classification scheme's primary function is to arrange books on shelves, documents in files and so on; the same order

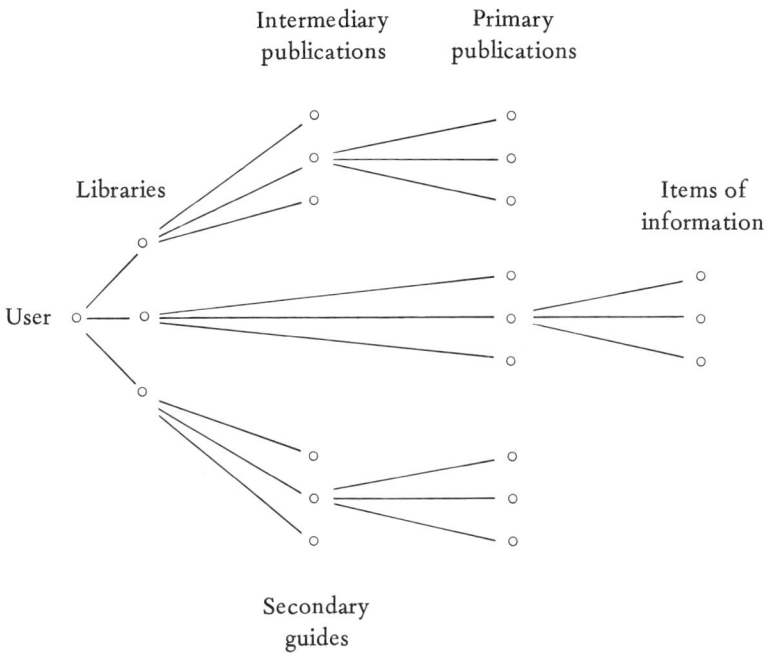

of subjects may also be used in an index to these collections, so that the order of the entries in the index corresponds to the order of the books and documents themselves. Even where an alphabetical order of subjects is preferred, there must be a scheme of cross-references to link related subjects or they will indeed lie in a disordered heap like peas in a bag.

The scheme should reflect the pattern of reality as closely as the current state of public information allows, because it aims at finding, not only a specific document asked for by its correct name, but also other documents that contain equally relevant information. These will most likely be by other authors, each with his own unique way of understanding the reality he is writing about. Indeed, it is only the reality that they are discussing that is shared by all these authors. It is inevitable that, as with all other representations of reality, classification schemes will in time become incapable of accurately accommodating the new information being made public. This is inevitable because any scheme has to be designed on the basis of what is taken to be the reality of things and the relations between them at a particular era. We are very familiar, in this country, with the way in which aggregations of new discoveries finally tend to break up accepted patterns of thought. When this happens, there is no alternative but to remake at least that part of the system where the new paradigm has become accepted.

Since this happens all the time, both the Decimal Classification Office and the UDC office have staff constantly engaged in making revisions. But it is a matter for some astonishment that librarians can accept very happily the prospect of spending many millions of pounds, and enduring great upheavals, in order to move into new buildings, but are very reluctant to spend any money or effort in revising classifications.

Each part of the field of knowledge, moreover, does not exist in isolation any more than an individual fact. The interaction and interpenetration of phenomena goes on all the time, in such a variety of circumstances that if we were unable to classify, we should remain in a constant state of utter bewilderment. For example, steel structures may be corroded by sulphur dioxide fumes in the air, and by bacteria; bacteria may cause corrosion of steel structures, and disease; disease may be caused by bacteria, and by bad housing conditions; bad housing conditions may be due to the corrosion of steel structures. Bad housing conditions may also contribute to the production of great literature – the poet in the garret; sulphur dioxide fumes may lead to the promotion of legislation; disease may lead to an awakening of religious feeling.

Nothing can be said to be peculiar to one context, and while a classification scheme may locate the names of things in the most appropriate class, it must also provide a means for indicating relationships between different classes. The same applies to processes: relations such as cause, influence, control, deterioration, may exist in almost any field of knowledge, and even between fields that have hitherto appeared to be unconnected.

When approaching a retrieval system, an externalized memory, with a request for information, the user hopes to find a structure or order which makes sense to him in that he can relate it to a pattern in his own mind, his own point of view. He first of all puts into words what he conceives to be the subject on which he requires information. This is a considerable mental discipline, and it is well known to librarians that users rarely succeed in stating their requirements with any precision. They usually ask for a broader subject, a 'main class', and so run the risk of recalling masses of information that is relevant but not pertinent and may even be confusing.

This is a phenomenon that we might expect. When a user has been stimulated to make a reference search, it means that he has become aware of a gap in his knowledge. He wants new information, or maybe information that he once knew but has forgotten – it has lapsed from his own memory and he needs recourse to a record. He finds that he has only an anomalous state of information, that the sum of what he knows of a particular subject does not make a complete or coherent picture; something is lacking. The word or words that he chooses to state his need are more likely to describe the part of the subject that he does know, because he is probably unsure about the missing pieces. It is hard for him to do otherwise, since a considerable mental effort is required to visualize and describe clearly the nature of what one does not know. The fact that something is lacking impresses itself clearly and urgently enough, but the shape and size of the gap are vague and often simply cannot be known at all.

The outcome of this uncertainty is that the user is liable to choose a word that is different from the word used in the library's indexes for the subject he wants. The index refers him to certain documents and these are not what he wants; they are, so to speak, impertinent. Unless the index has a classified structure leading him to the right words, he either assumes that there are no documents on his subject, in which case the system has let him down; or he has to search again in his own memory, to make another guess, knowing that the word he chose was wrong, but not knowing how. The system has not supplemented his memory, but remained silent.

The same applies to a librarian mediating between the user and the system, and Melvil Dewey and most of his successors have striven to introduce mnemonic principles into their classification schemes.

The motive that inspired these compilers was to provide each librarian with a key to his own stock, by indexing the subjects it covered and arranging the contents in a useful order corresponding to the way in which experts thought about their own specialities. Interestingly enough, Dewey himself stated in his first edition of 1876 that his own scheme was devised for cataloguing and indexing purposes, but was found to be equally valuable for numbering and arranging books and pamphlets on the shelves. It was actually entitled 'A Classification and Subject Index'. The authors of the great Library of Congress scheme, eschewing both philosophical and mnemonic principles, arranged their books on the shelves first and wrote out the schedules afterwards. The result is a large and wasteful scheme inflexibly tied to the general state of knowledge around the turn of the century.

Through the effectiveness of the national inter-library lending system based on the National Central Library, librarians in Britain had for long been accustomed to drawing more widely from their own stock in answering subject enquiries, and many other systems for promoting local co-operation exist, in which public, university and special libraries form a local network with shared access to books and periodicals. The publication of the *British national bibliography* as a classified catalogue with a detailed and highly refined subject index gave a great impetus to such co-operation because its structure makes subject searches easy to carry out. Choosing a term in the subject index leads not only to books classified at that term in the schedules, but to an array of books classified under related terms, and the searcher who may have chosen the wrong term is helped to think further by the display of a structure of relationships between terms.

Subject catalogues arranged in alphabetical order of the terms, without the benefit of a classified display, have always been more popular in the United States, and several lists of preferred terms, Subject Headings, exist. Subject catalogues of the Library of Congress use their own Library of Congress Subject Headings, and these are now used to indicate the subjects of books listed on the computer tapes of the MARC Project for the machine-readable catalogues of the Library of Congress and the British National Bibliography. The tapes are widely available for use by other libraries, but the most satisfactory ways of using them have not yet been fully worked out.

What concerns me here, however, is not the fact of the existence of these and other automated catalogues, but the ways in which these systems deal with subject enquiries and literature searches. This comes back to the structure of the indexing language. One of the early results of the introduction of searching on machine-readable files was the abandoning of all schemes for controlling the choice of terms used for indexing, on the grounds that the computer's ability to search large stores at high speed made it easy enough to search and search again for a succession of words until the searcher hit upon the right one. No attempt was made even to link synonyms.

The great advantage claimed for this approach is that it is very cheap and efficient at the input stage. Free text indexing means that the indexer need not refer to any controlled vocabulary, such as a list of Subject Headings, but can simply use as entry points the terms used in a document being indexed. Anyone who has ever made or used the index to a book knows well enough that this may be cheap and easy for the indexer, but is the reverse for the user. Once again, choosing the wrong word may lead nowhere and the index provides no further help.

A more positive disadvantage is illustrated by a computer-produced type of index called Keyword-in-Context, or KWIC. This is produced very quickly by using the titles of the documents indexed, with one title per line of index. Each title is moved to and fro across the page so as to bring each significant, or key, word in the title to the centre of the page in turn; the list of titles is arranged in alphabetical order of keywords. Synonyms are separated: in one index of this type, titles using the words 'abroad', 'foreign' and 'overseas', synonyms in this particular index, are separated from each other by several pages of titles on other subjects.

The danger of this is not so much that the choice of one of those words only reveals a part of the information actually in the index, though this is a serious drawback. More insidious is the snare lurking in the fact that the user who finds titles under one of these words thinks he has found all that the index has to offer, and looks no further. The index has not only failed to help him think more efficiently, it has succeeded in stopping his thinking altogether. Free text indexing may be simple, but free text searching presents many problems which may not be at first apparent.

Recognition of this has led to a great revival of interest in lists of terms for special subjects, no longer called a Subject Headings list, except by the Library of Congress, but a 'thesaurus'. The history of some of these, such as the ERIC Thesaurus of the United States National Institute of Education (given in detail, with many others, in A C Foskett's *Subject approach to information*), shows an entertaining account of a losing battle against the use of classification, unwilling and sometimes incompetent.

The most efficient thesauri are certainly those which rely on the technique of facet analysis, though most of the compilers of thesauri do not recognize a debt to Ranganathan or even Roget. The basic principle is the same, that of dividing the terms from a subject field into a series of separate categories, each representing one particular facet of the field, and based on its internal logical structure. In a technology, we should expect to find facets for Product, Material, Process, Tool, Agent, and so on, and the relationship of these both to the logic of the subject and to Ranganathan's Fundamental Categories is easy to see. In Education, we find Persons (being educated), Schools, Curriculum Subjects, Teaching Methods, Teachers, plus a series of contributory foundation subjects such as Psychology, Sociology, Administration, Comparative studies.

The listing of terms in each facet takes the form of a traditional classification scheme, arranging classes by means of various relations to express subordination and co-ordination. The alphabetical section of the modern thesaurus somewhat resembles that of Roget, but a more or less standard form of expressing the relations to be found in the classified section has emerged, indicated by symbols such as SN, USE, UF, BT, NT, RT.

SN	Scope Note	provides a definition or description of the term used as the heading
USE or 'See . . .'		meaning that the term is not used in the classification
UF	Use for	the reciprocal of USE, indicating that this term is used in the classification
BT	Broader term	indicating a term in the classification with a wider range of meaning
NT	Narrower term	indicating a term with a narrower meaning

RT   Related term   indicating terms with a similar range of meaning, or co-ordinates, or other terms often found associated in the literature.

As experience in retrospective searching on a computer file has grown, so there has developed a widespread recognition, in specialized and scholarly fields at least, of the power of a thesaurus to improve efficiency in carrying out the action of giving a more or less precise statement of the enquiry being made. This can be done by consultation between librarian and enquirer, using the thesaurus, before keying in to a computerized data base, so achieving a great saving in connect time and avoiding frustration and disappointment. The more refined the thesaurus, the more effective the search strategy, and the moderate results obtained from more primitive search languages can be seen in the much trumpeted general systems such as Prestel and Ceefax.

The benefits of harmonizing a classification scheme and a thesaurus can be seen in the major work undertaken for Unesco by Jean Aitchison, whose long experience in thesaurus construction has consistently relied on faceted structured classification. She has based this thesaurus on the schedules of the new edition of the Bliss Bibliographic Classification compiled by Jack Mills at the Polytechnic of North London, and published in sections by Butterworths.

Having the ability to codify relationships and the association of ideas provides an equally essential basis for the other major aspect of information service, current awareness, often called Selective Dissemination of Information, SDI. While such a service may have existed in some libraries for years, sensible use of a computer can make it far more systematic, and combine it with the regular function of indexing new material as it reaches the library.

The service relies on close co-operation, between the library and its users, and the willingness of users to provide the library with a key to their interests, a profile made up of significant terms such as those used in a specialized thesaurus. As new documents, books, periodicals, reports, and so forth, arrive, they are scanned, their subject relevances identified, and a notice of their arrival sent to all users likely to be interested. This service, in any of its forms, can be carried out quite easily without a computer, providing that the library is sufficiently well staffed with qualified information people who can look at the new publications with expert eyes and identify their relevance. The 'list of current accessions' produced by many special and university libraries is an example of the shotgun approach, published in the knowledge that, since the library reflects the special and academic interests of its users, all new additions to the stock are likely to interest at least some of them.

The modern SDI service goes much farther than this, because it aims at achieving a more or less precise match with the users' interests. It is for this reason that the recording of interest profiles has taken on so great an importance. The general list takes for granted that all members of a particular institution will share the same broad spectrum of interests, and it is to the advantage of all members, including the library staff themselves, if the institution keeps at the forefront of its field because its members always have possession of the most up-to-date information.

The individual service has the same general aim, but in addition sets out to provide specialists with items bearing directly on their specialisms. In the first place, therefore, their profiles must be drafted with great accuracy, including fine detail if thought necessary. In the second place, the library's own indexers must be able to classify new material with the same precision, to avoid as far as possible all dangers of mismatching. The ability of computers to deal with detailed comparisons very quickly makes it possible to operate an SDI service with great refinement. The profiles are stored in a user file; new items are given keywords from the same lists as the profiles and these are entered in a bibliographic data file. The two files are matched and notices printed out for all hits.

This makes possible a considerable enlargement of the librarian's role as an active partner in the communication process. He no longer sits quietly at the information desk, as in the film, waiting for someone to ask a question, for all the world like one of Professor B F Skinner's pigeons. (On the whole, as Paul Weiss once remarked, people are not pigeons.) He has a positive function in relation to the community which established the library. He acts rather as the spotter in an aeroplane, who can see what goes on in the whole of a field beneath him because he does not have to attend in detail to any of its parts. By scanning all current additions with the whole range of users' interests in mind, he applies his skill in indexing to establishing direct communication between author and reader, detecting relevance in even the most obscure or unexpected publications.

So far from reducing the role of librarian to that of a machine minder, these activities place the library at the centre of the community of users. The ability of the human mind to associate new ideas with existing patterns of thought provides the motive power for advancing civilization. By analogy, the library acts as an externalized social memory on the one hand, and shows social sensitivity to new information on the other, and users of a library offering these services are enabled to sharpen their awareness of the world and its problems, and concentrate their minds on finding solutions. This places a heavy responsibility on the library and information profession; accepting it will involve the development of new skills and a positive approach to improving the old.

Chapter 9

LOOKING FOR ANSWERS

From this contemplation of the nature of library services in the context of culture and communication, several interesting contradictions emerge. They begin in educational controversy, where some dynamic and forward-looking persons have commented on the failure of schools and universities to fit their students for the stern reality of contemporary life. The academic tradition, they say, has separated young people from society, and given them a training suited only to passing examinations; selected pupils are interviewed on television to pronounce that school is only boring and life outside is more exciting. These critics are well placed to give such considered judgements, being themselves products of the academic tradition which has enabled them to reach positions from which they can make public statements.

The academic tradition turns out to be rooted in the study, not of real life, but of books. This will surprise many authors, who thought that they wrote about real life as they themselves experienced it and felt their experience had enough human value to be worth communicating to other people. In a lecture to the Royal Society of Arts, Dr J A Pope, speaking on 'The role of the universities in a changing, technologically based industrial society', naturally stressed the social value of engineers, being an engineer himself. He went on, however, to criticize university teaching for relying too much on what he called 'book-learning'. He did not specify how much is 'too much', and no doubt we can all agree that 'too much' of anything is not good. Even engineers must rely sometimes on information in books. I suspect that what Dr Pope had in mind was not so much book-learning, of which I have no doubt that he himself has plenty, but rote-learning — the sort of learning which contradicts everything a library stands for, and in which large numbers of isolated facts have to be committed to memory and reproduced under the sudden-death circumstances of examinations, like the unhappy candidates in A C Hilton's immortal parody, *The vulture and the husbandman*, who stand for university examiners:

> They answered everything they could,
> And wrote with all their might,
> But, though they wrote it all by rote,
> They did not write it right.

But, says the argument, the academic tradition does not relate to real life, and books are academic, so books do not relate to real life either. The academic curriculum, says one academic research worker, has drawn far more from the library than from 'the factory or the hospital or the marketplace', when it ought to have been preparing for the realities of life. One is inclined to wonder whether this scholar's children gain their education from these admirable and necessary places, all of which, it will be noted, are concerned only with the material basis for staying alive.

Pressing forward with our contradictions, we come back to the old controversy, between librarian and information officer, the basis being that, as their name implies, librarians are concerned with the handling of books as physical objects. Information officers are members of a team consisting of several specialists, and their role is to be users of information and providers of information to the rest of the team. They are not concerned with managing collections of books. In any case, information technology, it is claimed, will bring about the demise of libraries, except for archives, says one, or light fiction, says another (both, as it happens, doctors of philosophy).

I have no doubts whatever about the essential character of an information service and the vital part that the service plays in the advancement of learning. I believe quite firmly in the function of an information specialist and in the nature of information science as analysed, for example, by Vickery. I do not believe that this involves a total separation from the practice of librarianship in its modern sense, and when I look at the real world, I see that, in fact, this is not the case. When a new paradigm appears, it does not result in the total rejection of the old, but takes from it what is still valuable. Physicists were physicists before and after Einstein and Niels Bohr. Their view of the subject was enlarged, not destroyed. Let us remember that Newton said that if he had been able to see farther than others, it was because he stood on the shoulders of giants.

This particular contradiction seems all the more regrettable therefore, in that it creates tensions between groups of professional people who should be natural allies in the preservation and development of the cultural heritage.

All four contradictions, indeed, are 'academic' in the unreal sense that books are academic and the academic tradition is ignorant of real life. Of course no one in their right mind has ever claimed, or would ever claim, that life can be understood solely from books, or even from periodicals or reports from the Atomic Energy Authority. No one who has a mind to enhance human culture can claim that it can be done without books — not as archives or light fiction, though these have a part to play, but as the embodiment of considered judgements in every field. John Ziman, professor of theoretical physics and Fellow of the Royal Society, inveighs against 'information retrieval' in the sense of non-stop collection of mere factual data without pausing to reflect and consider what sort of pattern emerges: 'To neglect the writing of monographs and treatises, to treat this as somehow not 'research work' like watching meters and scribbling algebra ... is to betray the scientific tradition. To find something out, look first in a book, not the abstracts!'

Science and, one might add, all other fields of knowledge, need analytically ordered and coherent systems of ideas every bit as much as the accumulation of details — probably more, when we consider how much detail has been accumulated and how necessary it is, at the present crisis in history, for the powerful and the decision-makers actually to have ordered and coherent systems of ideas in their minds. Many public pronouncements from these quarters indicate that this need is becoming urgent and ought to be met.

It will not, however, be met by the total neglect of libraries. This will not happen unless we wish to realize the *1984* of Orwell or the brave new world of Aldous Huxley. It might happen here, though, if librarians overreact to the multitude of papers announcing the paperless society, and become mere removals men in the information age, forgetting that moving bits of information from here to there does not by itself result in the building of coherent structures. The profession of librarianship, and the genuine contribution it has to make to the information age, will not survive if it abandons its commitment to the cultural heritage. The accumulation of details forms an integral part; the task of improving the flow of information about details is vital; they are means to an end, not an end in themselves.

The case for a contribution from professional librarianship rests on a wider range of skills than mere 'information processing', the moving of bits from here to there, without regard to the reasons why such removals may be necessary. An encouraging indication of official recognition of this potential lies in the reconstitution and re-naming of the advisory body for the Minister for Arts and Libraries; from being the Library Advisory Council with an academic chairman, it has become the Library and Information Services Council with the former Director of Sheffield University Department of Information Studies as Chairman, Professor W L Saunders, whose contribution to education for an integrated profession can scarcely be overestimated. In Annual Reports to Parliament, the Minister himself has drawn attention to the dangers of reducing support for libraries, because we need the contribution they make to the well-being and progress of the country.

To justify the Minister's confidence, the practice of librarians, and of information scientists, will need to demonstrate that there is indeed more to it than information transfer. I have repeatedly stressed the importance of this, but this is, of course, precisely the area in which machines can provide most help. The act of putting an enquiry to a data base is purely clerical — that of tapping out a series of letters or figures on the keyboard; any skilled typist can quickly learn to operate a terminal. Since this is the case, there seems to me to be as little justification for claiming that this requires professional training as there is in making the same claim for stamping dates on the label in a book.

Neither of these processes requires the professional education that characterizes, or ought to characterize, the librarians and information scientists whose activities are required for the well-being and progress of the country. It would be very unwise for them to base any claim for due recognition on such simple skills. As we know, because we are constantly being told by manufacturers, everyone's ambition should be directed towards home ownership of a computer. The fact that most of the persuasion is based on the ability to play games, or have instant information on the results of horse races and football matches, gives some indication of what these manufacturers think about the minds of their prospective customers. Librarians are accustomed to this, as only a few computer salesmen have the faintest idea of the real relationship between information and the serious enquirer, with whom librarians themselves are familiar.

What raises the use of a terminal above the clerical level is, of course, the intellectual preparation, whether this be the work of a skilled intermediary assisting in the interrogation of one or more of the large public data bases, or the executive of a large corporation holding an on-line enquiry into some urgent aspect of the corporation's business. In every case, a specific question, or a highly focused discussion and set of questions, is the result of distilling the essence of a much wider range of personal knowledge, and concentrating information into a form that a machine can understand.

One would have thought it to be obvious that the advances in computer manufacture made possible by the silicon chip would immediately have brought the on-line access facility into the realm of home ownership, as the portable typewriter has enabled many to produce correspondence that is easily legible. In principle, and probably in practice as well, the ability to use a microcomputer to access data bases should become commonplace, and have no more effect on libraries than the ability to buy books to read at home. The essential skill of the librarian lies not in the processes involved in lending books across a counter, any more than the skill of a pharmacist lies in reading doctors' handwriting and putting pills into boxes.

Understanding the function and the techniques for organizing information transfer systems goes much deeper, and should lead to increased and improved use of machines to increase and improve the value of libraries, not to lead to their extinction. The industrial executive holding a conference by means of an in-house network does not dream up a business meeting on the spur of the moment, a sudden impulse to see and talk to others on his terminal. He has to know the history of his firm, the nature of its products, the technical and marketing problems and so forth; in short, he has to have an ordered and coherent picture of everything that has gone before and makes this conference necessary. In the same way, the user of a data base, like the user of a library, has a mental picture, from which something missing provides the necessary motivation for looking at a store of information to supply it. The extent to which the store has itself an ordered and coherent structure determines the success of the enquiry.

Such a structure results from nothing less than expert cataloguing and classification. Whatever words may be used, the process of making a description of a document, or any piece of information, giving it a recognized and recognizable name, and linking its subject with the same and related subjects in other documents, constitutes one of the basic skills of what we call librarianship. To claim, as some have done, that the application of these techniques, and of all librarianship, is limited to books, or print on paper, betrays an ignorance of library practice that would be ludicrous if it did not seem to be wilful misrepresentation. It is, on the contrary, precisely these skills that lift the computer interrogation process above the clerical task of keyboard operation. The intellectual preparation comprises two main aspects: the first is the identification as exactly as possible of the object of the search, that is the subject on which the enquirer seeks further information. This relates to the mental act of classifying the enquiry. The second aspect consists of two steps: identifying the data base or bases that are likely to provide the answer, and then translating the terms of the enquiry into the terms used by the indexers who input the information into the data base in the first place.

Knowledge of reference sources and where to find them has always been the stamp of the experienced librarian. The librarian, of whatever library, said Jean Baptiste Cotton des Houssayes in his address to the general assembly of the Sorbonne on the 23rd of December, 1780, will be a stranger to no part of the field of knowledge. And the identification of the data base appropriate to search for particular information is no less part of the librarian's trade than the identification of a book or article from a printed catalogue or bibliography. The Central Information Service of the University of London has produced the popular *LUCIS guide*, which is a printed catalogue, with annotations of data bases available on-line from the Service, and forms an essential aid for the many regular users of the Service.

Translating the subject of an enquiry into the terms used to find subjects in a data base is usually, and most effectively, done by consulting a thesaurus. The indexing of most data bases at the input stage is often done by means of the indexing system's own thesaurus. One of the largest and best known is the Thesaurus of *Engineering and scientific terms* (TEST) produced by the Engineers Joint Council with the United States Department of Defense, and its object is 'to produce a comprehensive thesaurus of scientific and technical terms for use as a basic reference in information storage and retrieval systems and to provide a vocabulary groundwork by means of which the interchange of information might be enhanced'.

Great schemes like this, and Jean Aitchison's *Thesaurofacet* produced for the English Electric Company, do indeed provide valuable compendia useful in defining search strategies for a wide range of computerized and non-computerized indexes. *Thesaurofacet* has become a model for many successors, and displays very well the structural advantage to be gained by incorporating facet analysis into the basic organization of the list of terms. It has value as a formal vocabulary useful for specifying enquiry subjects in a computerized search even though it was not produced originally for use with any public data base.

The majority of searches on a terminal do not end with the visual display. In most cases, the visual display does not answer an enquiry, but refers the enquirer to sources which do. The first search term may elicit the fact that there are hundreds, even thousands, of references; successively added terms in combination narrow this down eventually to a manageable number, when it may be reasonable to obtain a printout of all of them. A preliminary routine asks the computer to display the titles and/or the abstracts of three or four, which can probably all be read on the screen at the same time. This display tells whether the searcher is on the right lines, in producing relevant references; it may, on occasion, actually provide all the information the searcher requires. If it does not, the searcher has to take the next step, which is, of course, to consult the documents to which the references refer. Usually, these will come from a library in the shape of books and periodicals.

A successful search like this, with a minimum of expensive connect time actually interrogating the data base on-line, results from the exercise of considerable skill in both aspects of the intellectual preparation. Just as the great increase in the number of print-on-paper documents was an important factor in the development of the information officer function, notably in industry, so the similar growth in the number and complexity of computerized data bases makes it probable that a similar 'intermediary' function will be required by most users. Most research workers and scholars are familiar with a few core reference works and indexes which they can use without the need for assistance; most scientists can search *Chemical abstracts* more or less efficiently. They do not expect to have to devote a lot of time to acquiring the same expertise in using many others. They do expect to be able to consult a skilled intermediary for assistance outside of their own limited range.

I believe that this will apply even to those who invest in a home microcomputer. There is, without doubt, an attraction is using one of these gadgets, and the proud owner will certainly want to derive the utmost benefit from it. It seems that an occupational hazard is developing, indeed, and that the attraction may become an obsession. The insidious tendency of means to become ends will begin to exert its baleful influence. It must be resisted, otherwise the slave becomes the master. But Gutenberg's invention did not eliminate the live lecture, even though books became cheap and easily available, and television has not so far replaced live performance in a theatre. There has grown up a wholly desirable co-operation between the media. Books have resulted from television series like those of Kenneth Clark and Bronowski, and books have very often provided the texts for television and radio programmes, or given a full picture of events which have had only instant presentations in progammes of news. It heartens one to see the Librarian of the Pepys Library in Cambridge, Mr Robert Latham, being interviewed on the notable occasion of the completion of his edition of the *Diary*, and giving an entertaining account of the background in the life of the time. This could not be done by the book alone, any more than television can present the full flavour of the *Diary*. Each presentation enhances the other.

Librarians should therefore welcome the opportunities offered by new technology for improving rather than attacking the use of libraries. Properly used, computers can open up new avenues of approach to great works given permanent value through print. Even the video disc, with its great storage capacity and flexibility of use, cannot equal the book or article in their ability to present a coherent and reasoned argument, because the flow of thought is there on the page; the reader can pause to reflect, can skip back and forth. The book, in short, presents a coherent structure of thinking, and not just a visual image.

Neither can a machine, however sophisticated, provide the inter-personal relationship which is an essential foundation for all human communication. If this were not so, the communication would not be human, which is characterized by the interplay of minds which have a great deal in common in their life histories but which yet denote unique personalities. However well programmed, in the act of interrogation the computer terminal can act as a mirror to the mind of the user, because it acts only on a stimulus from the user. Certainly the file can incorporate the sort of relationships illustrated by a thesaurus, but it is only capable of producing information through tracks already laid down, and the user has a 'dialogue' with himself, unless aided by interaction with another human mind. However advanced the machines of the future may become, the human personality will always be a step ahead, because it is the human mind which creates the machine, and not the other way about.

We cannot achieve a full measure of self-enhancement, especially that revival and refreshment of the human spirit which we call recreation, by relying solely on our own resources; unless we have communication with other minds, we are bound to fall short of realizing our own potential. Such communication can be effected through a variety of media, but only by personal interaction can he feel the actual glow of sympathetic understanding that comes from shared experience of the human condition.

What machines can perform, often better than people, are the myriad of tedious and repetitive routines that are time-consuming and delay our arrival at ends that are clearly in view. Number crunching is a common and outstanding example. So is searching the literature over a number of years when no cumulative index is available in print. One of the splendid features of the public systems of data bases is the remarkable ease and speed with which we can move from one base to another in the same search. Like any other tool the computer gives of its best in the hands of a skilful craftsman. The combination of skilful handling and right judgement brings swift rewards from a computer search, and it is this combination which offers the most promise for future progress in information transfer.

The opposite of progress will occur if our efforts are stultified by nonsensical theories leading to stupid practice. If 'information' becomes reified into a commodity subject to the laws and forces involved in commodity production and distribution, there is a real danger that quality will be sacrificed to quantity, and the information industry will produce and process large quantities of rubbish in order to prove what vast quantities it can process. We do not have to belong to the dismal and defeatist school of 'more means worse' if we wish to oppose the apparently attractive but actually meretricious school of 'we must do it because we can'. Once more, means are in danger of becoming ends.

Failure to realize this important distinction now presents us with the spectacle of what is offered as a way out of a crisis leading to exactly the same crisis in a different form. The prophets of the paperless society claim to believe that progress is hampered by the production of too much paper, and that the busy executive and decision-maker has to spend so much time acquiring and reading documents of various kinds that his real work suffers. The speed and manoeuvreability of the computer saves much of this time and wasted effort. The in-house network avoids the use of in-house memoranda, and keeps the in-trays empty.

But if excess paper is replaced by an equal excess of visual display, where is the gain? Of course, some decision-making can be accelerated and this is all to the good. Where reflection and study are required, where what is needed is what we rightly call a 'more informed' judgement, then instant reactions do not meet the case at all. They will more likely lead to a 'snap' judgement, especially where the terminal announces another request for an instant conference. The telephone has led to a decrease in personal correspondence, which to me seems a doubtful advantage, but official letter-writing has contributed greatly to the overloading of officials. And how often does an executive, in business, government, education, answer his own telephone? The unrestrained proliferation of machine-based information transfer could well lead to a similar situation, and produce a new type of professional intermediary who acts as a barrier rather than an aid to communication, a filter rather than a channel, and who has much greater opportunity to stop or distort a message.

The advocates of unrestrained development always criticize this reasonable degree of caution on the grounds that only hardened reactionaries would wish to stand in the way of progress, that one must not hinder the march of science, and so forth. It seems to me that, on the contrary, an unrestrained proliferation of technology itself hinders the march of science. Science – and science is an essential ingredient of wisdom – can only progress when scientists have the opportunity to consider how new information relates to the present stock. The rest of us can only benefit from the march of science when the conclusions of such considerations are explained to us in terms that we can understand because they relate to our own experience. The same goes for politicians and other decision-makers. We all need time to consider how to deal with new information, and we cannot have this if we are constantly called on to look at new technical marvels, or our attention is constantly distracted by the appearance of more instant information on a VDU.

The essence of *1984, Brave new world* and similar futuristic tales of horror lies in the control of public communication by those who are not the end users of the controlled information. I suppose I should emphasize that, when I speak of the dangers of unrestrained proliferation of machine-based information transfer, I do not suggest that control of information should rest in the hands of officials whose activities are not subject to public scrutiny. I do not suggest, either, that we are entirely free of this sort of control even in democratic societies. I should prefer to see self-restraint, or self-control, which would no doubt be quite acceptable even to the most anarchically inclined.

Any scientist will maintain that high standards result from an agreed system of self-restraint working through professional judgements; in publication, the system of referees exemplifies this. Such judgements may sometimes be wrong, since no one, not even the most experienced and expert, can be right all the time. But they will always represent some kind of consensus based on professional and not solely personal considerations. Most professional organizations now promulgate codes of ethics or codes of practice, and rely on their members to uphold these codes in the interests of the community at large. In return, the members themselves gain from the support of the profession because of the community's recognition of its services.

It behoves a profession to organize itself and its practice so that the community can see it in action. Professional techniques, such as cataloguing and classification, information retrieval and dissemination, should never be allowed to become ends in themselves, however fascinating their study may appear. The community must be able to see that such techniques are put to use for the common good, and not for the self-aggrandisement of those who practise them. And the community must have evidence of a reasoned and balanced approach to the use and development of professional practices; a professional group can only bring discredit on itself if it appears to be blown hither and thither by the latest fashions, by undue exaggeration of the importance of this or that new toy, and by wholesale discarding of what the community sees as still valuable.

The profession of librarianship and information science organizes itself at several levels and covers a wide range of functions and techniques. Experience in recent years shows how these interrelate: archivists at what has traditionally been thought of as the historical end of a spectrum now join hands with records officers in the heart of information officer territory in business and government. Through the work of national associations, standards and codes of practice help to shape and regulate professional activity, and co-operative actions help to influence opinion in the public mind and even in the seats of power. At the international level, the IFLA programmes of Universal Bibliographic Control and Universal Availability of Publications form twin peaks of achievement, scaled after many years of unsuccessful attempts, and immensely stimulated by the possibilities of automation.

My earlier criticisms of the lack of reference to library and information services at the two Unesco Conferences, on Books and on Cultural Policies, seem all the more unfortunate when one remembers all the past efforts of Unesco to promote a professional approach backed up by genuine commitment on the part of the governments of member states. In 1974, after a long period of preparation through a series of regional meetings, Unesco convened a conference on infrastructures for National Library and Information Services, which announced the programme called NATIS. This was intended to encourage national governments to establish or strengthen their own networks of libraries of all kinds, particularly in those most closely involved with scientific and technical development programmes. This would effect a big improvement in the basic resources available for the already existing UNISIST.

Both UNISIST and NATIS now come within the purview of the General Information Programme which, although it has national committees, rarely seems to emerge into the public gaze; one would have expected that, at least at the World Congress on Books, the GIP representative would have made some impact in view of the success of UNISIST. It is urgently necessary that the barriers between all groups engaged in communication should be broken down, so that each group can put a right value on the work of the others. Even in a democratic society, some planning at the national level is required if international efforts are to succeed, and this can only be achieved by professional co-operation and co-ordination. Better communication with each other can only result in better communications for the rest of the community.

Chapter 10

A READING SOCIETY

We live in one world but, as the MacBride Commission says, we hear many voices. Over the centuries, human ingenuity has constantly been directed towards improving ways to ensure that these voices shall be heard, ever more clearly and ever more quickly. Harnessing the energy of atoms and electrons has annihilated distance, and the one world has become a global village. Instant information on events thousands of miles away has become available in sound and vision.

One might have hoped that such an increase in the quantity of information available about our global neighbours would result in better understanding and global harmony. The 140 wars that have been fought since 1945 show that this is unfortunately not the case, and it is not difficult to see why. Even when we are apparently informed by seeing what happens as it happens, we actually receive only a two-dimensional picture, and the full story never reaches us. The conflict between Britain and Argentina over a few remote islands in the South Atlantic proves beyond doubt that such reporting is partial, biassed, incomplete and often misleading. The facts may speak for themselves, but that is all they do speak for. Subsequent reporting and discussion testify to the extra fact that more questions have been asked than answered.

This does not deny the value of instant information. If it had been available from W H Russell, the suffering of the troops and the achievements of Florence Nightingale would have been known much sooner from the Crimean War – merely a foolish expedition to the Black Sea, made for no sufficient reason, in G M Trevelyan's opinion. Advances in technology certainly can bring us the facts with the speed of light and this is greatly to be desired. What we should strive to ensure, however, is not that this great facility should be used merely to transfer more and more information, but that the time saved should be put to the more vital purpose of promoting understanding through more considered judgements and more effective communication.

The mere statement of factual information does not of itself constitute communication, and communication is what the world needs. Many voices all speaking at once announce their messages to no avail if no one listens. Communication involves sharing of information and unless sharing takes place there is no communication. Much play is made, especially by journalists from Western countries, on the need for a 'free flow of information' between nations and, once again, no one can expose themselves as against such a free flow. But two factors have to be taken into account. The first is that some censorship exists everywhere, whether overt through a government office or concealed through private ownership and control of the media.

The second factor is that any flow of information, free or controlled, has to be directed towards some receiver if the information is to be communicated. The root cause of problems in communication, with which the MacBride Commission was concerned, seems to me to lie in the way that producers of information ignore this factor, and take little or no account of the real information needs of the receivers. Facts are launched, literally now, into space in the knowledge that modern technology makes it easy for anyone to bring them down to earth again, regardless of whether there is any benefit to be gained by so doing. Some members of the MacBride Commission, especially those from Third World countries, strongly emphasized that they have in practice no choice — their own countries are short of the means to produce and disseminate their own information, their own versions of events, their own points of view. They are forced to rely on what countries with advanced technology choose to send, for example through organizations such as Reuter and the Associated Press.

Communication in its proper sense of sharing information ought to be a two-way process, otherwise it can easily turn into 'cultural imperialism', against which Brandt and many other reports have warned. The culture which every people has the right and the duty to develop should not be allowed, still less forced, to degenerate into a pale imitation of the culture of countries rich enough to have the will and the technology to ensure that it is their culture and values that are globally distributed. A free flow of information should flow freely in both directions, and this means that all countries should have the opportunity to make their voices heard, in the knowledge that someone is listening. How this can be done poses many large questions, of course, but libraries can make a significant contribution in their role of safeguarding the records of culture and making them available.

Sharing information through genuine, two-way communication develops understanding of, and sympathy with, the ways and values of others, and the more effective the communication, the more chance people have to live in harmony and peace with one another. Human nature is shaped by the sort of society we live in, and the practices and objectives which go to form its moral values. Human practice requires, of necessity, a publicly available stock of information from which to devise means to cope with the environment, and in doing so, men consciously evolve purposes and goals which are social and so require them to work and plan together. The present age has seen the extension of the possibility to do this on the international scale — technology has given us both the weapons to engage in nuclear war and the opportunity to reach international agreement to prevent it. Real communication aimed at reaching such agreement is necessary if we wish to achieve the purpose to keep humanity going. When the fate of the world depends on the state of mind of a few individuals whose action consists merely of pressing buttons on a computer terminal, it surely becomes of considerable importance that those people should not only know a lot of facts, but also have the time and opportunity to reflect on them, and discuss them with others. Communication involves the sharing of points of view as well as of facts, and this means more than making statements ('speeches') to each other. Sharing of points of view also contributes to the evolving of common aims and purposes, and a reduction of tension and hostility.

Thus the end, or aim, of information transfer is not achieved simply by taking bits of information from a tape or disc and displaying them on a VDU. This can never be more than one part of a process by means of which an individual can enter into the world of publicly available information and assimilate relevant items, or 'interiorize' them in Michael Polanyi's phrase, into the private stock of knowledge which he already possesses. The world of his own conscious experience is enlarged by entry into what Karl Popper has called World 3, the world of 'objective knowledge' which is available for anyone to acquire. In Popper's scheme, World 1 consists of the physical world in which we actually live, World 2 consists of subjective knowledge gained through conscious experience, and World 3 consists of the logical content of theories and the discussions, difficulties and problems that arise from them. These are published in journals and books and stored in libraries. Every subjective act of understanding is anchored in this World 3 and consists of operations with the 'objects' found in it, almost as if they were actual physical objects from World 1. 'Instead of growing better memories and brains, we grow paper, pens, pencils, typewriters, dictaphones, the printing press, and libraries. These add to our language — and especially to its descriptive and argumentative functions — what may be described as new dimensions. The latest development (used mainly in support of our argumentative abilities) is the growth of computers'.

Not everyone agrees with Popper's general conclusions about the nature of science, and it has been pointed out that he can be inconsistent: that he is certain, for example, that there is no such thing as certain knowledge. But what he says about World 3 seems to me to show sufficient insight into the actual working of library and information services to assist in developing ideas about their role in the modern world of information transfer and communication.

In order to demonstrate how this role might be played, one primary model of the information transfer process describes four stages in the use of a library to satisfy a need for information

1 Awareness — the user acquires a first insight into the nature of the service and makes an approach to it.

2 Attitude formation — the response received encourages the user to avail himself of the service.

3 Trial/decision — the favourable result of a trial decides the user that the service meets his need.

4 Confirmation — regular and systematic use of the service confirms the decision, or may reverse it if the service fails.

The importance of this model is that it not only suggests, but requires, a positive interaction between the supplier and the user of the service, and the information which the user seeks relates directly to his practice. The process of transfer is mediated through language. One of Popper's critics, Maurice Cornforth, stresses that successful practice depends largely on the validity of the information availabe: 'The *information which practice requires is communicable, and is expressed in sentences and conveyed by language* ... people formulate and communicate information about objects to inform and guide their practice'.

The history of practice in a community, and the comments that its members make on that practice, constitute the cultural heritage, embodied as 'Objective knowledge' and stored in libraries. Libraries cannot act so irresponsibly as to neglect their role as repositories; if they did, their community would be in danger of losing its cultural heritage altogether. Objective knowledge exists as a product of human activity, the record of successful (and unsuccessful) practice; human activity in turn leads to a new awareness of 'anomalous states' of information, the lack of something which someone else may have discovered and recorded; such records are themselves objective knowledge; consulting them in a library leads to improvements in human activity, and so the cultural heritage progresses.

By making the past serve the present in this cycle, libraries occupy one of the key positions in the communication process. The lack of any significant reference to this in documents like MacBride and the World Conference reports arises, I suggest, from the general belief that while libraries are admirable institutions, they and their keepers are not concerned with the active side of communication. This, it is said, rests with the journalists, editors, radio and television pundits, who give the public what they think it ought to have. Librarians, on the other hand, give the public what it asks for, and are concerned with the passive side of the process, and do not engage themselves in the positive act of communication. Librarians certainly enjoy public esteem, but this arises from their reputation as collectors and preservers rather than exploiters of the records under their control. Hence the desire of information officers, who are concerned with active exploitation, to consider themselves a separate profession entitled to higher status. This is not altogether surprising when one remembers the number of university tutors who appear to look on librarianship as the ideal career for a student recovering from a nervous breakdown and in need of a quiet life.

Unfortunately, some librarians acquiesce in this assumption of a passive role, and doubt whether they should go beyond collecting and preserving the records. Adopting this attitude seems to me to play into the hands of those who see no future for this profession. If a librarian has to do no more than sit at a desk waiting to be prompted into action to search out a record, a modern computer terminal can do this just as well, and in some cases better. It acts more quickly and is supposed not to make mistakes. If this were all, one could with equanimity view the future as a prospect of all one needs to know coming into the home via the TV screen — 'the micro at the breakfast table', as it were.

Herein lies the snare for those librarians also who are leaping on the bandwagon of Information Technology to the exclusion of the traditional role of collecting and preserving the cultural heritage, the objective knowledge recorded in books and documents. To imagine that a claim to professional status rests on total dedication to machine operations implies acquiescence in the prospect of the slave becoming the master, that the machine will control the librarian instead of the other way about. The extremist view that by the year 2000 libraries will have disappeared from the social scene except for a few institutions that preserve the printed records of the past, as passive archives, would be ludicrous if it were not highly dangerous. There is a danger to the profession of librarian, in that users with home terminals can have direct access to the public data bases without the necessity of an intermediary. If the future librarian's claim to social status rests on mere technical expertise, it is as if the future of the motorcar depended on everyone becoming a full-time mechanic instead of an owner-driver who uses a car to move from place to place. Even today, the 'Intelibot' at Kanazawa Industrial University in Japan, can pick tapes from a store and slot them into a player, in response to students who only have to punch in the tape number and wait for it to appear on their screen.

The disappearance of libraries and librarians would not endanger humanity if communication were merely a matter of moving bits of information from place to place. The sort of technical expertise required would be analogous to that of the motor mechanic whose objective is to ensure that the machine works; he has no interest in starting points or destinations. Likewise, the librarian as no more than a technical expert will be concerned only with the efficiency of the computer in the process of data transfer. The implications of this view for society constitute a far more worrying outlook than the situation of the library profession. Society does not exist in order to provide employment for any profession.

What is much more dangerous is that the whole concept of Information Technology in this narrow sense means the development of a society which is thoroughly superficial in its attitude to knowledge, and which has no stability because its existence depends, not on the security of the shared points of view which add up to a cultural heritage, but on a continuous flow of separate bits of information. The individual will have no time or opportunity to digest and assimilate all these separate bits, or to build them into a coherent and integrated structure. Society will become a behaviourist paradise, and human beings will behave as if they were machines only able to act in response to external stimuli. Power will reside in those who provide the stimuli, and unless they have the time and the will to form considered judgements, progress in the global village will consist in a succession of crisis responses to the latest bits of information, no matter what their source or validity.

The grain of truth that must be sifted from unromantic speculations about the paperless society of the future is that the traditions and practices of the library and information profession make a contribution that must be continued, adapted and improved. The significance of the 'information officer' concept lies not so much in the stress it puts on efficient technical processes such as classification, important though that is, but in the factor advanced as being distinct from librarianship: direct concern with the contents of documents and their value for specific groups of users. And it may seem that the stimulus for the development of information services lay in the nature of the contents: the 'neutrality' of scientific information, meaning that a scientist can rely on an intermediary to use the literature on his behalf, and developing countries can use information produced in advanced countries without having to repeat basic research themselves.

I do not believe that information services cannot operate in the social sciences and humanities. They are just as dependent on factual, or neutral, information as the sciences; a factual statement about the specific heat of mercury does not differ in kind from a factual statement about population growth or the authorship of Boswell's life of Samuel Johnson. But science is just as liable to controversy over value judgements as the humanities. The tone of arguments over Lysenko's theories on genetics does not differ greatly from that of certain arguments over the authorship of the plays attributed to Shakespeare. I see no reason why librarians should not venture to provide information services in these other fields; on the contrary, I believe very firmly that this is precisely the role that must be undertaken if the profession of librarianship is to maintain its contribution to a future society which values its cultural heritage and refuses to be reduced to mere fact-gathering. Librarians, being human themselves, can recognize value judgements as well as anyone else; indeed, their professional training ought to sharpen this faculty so that they can use it better in reader service. By the same token, librarians ought to develop a refined sensitivity and understanding of the human condition in order to promote a better use of imaginative literature in its function of conveying insight rather than factual data. Such insight into, and understanding of, the human condition is what humanity needs most urgently at the present time. We do not need a moratorium on scientific research, as some prophets of doom assert; neither do we need to be submerged under a deluge of trivial and repetitive facts, whether foisted on us by print on paper or electrons on a screen.

Information Technology has so much to offer in improving the lot of suffering humanity that it will be the greatest tragedy yet if we allow it to become an end in itself, and librarians have a unique part to play in preventing this. On no account should libraries degenerate into passive archives visited only by an ever-decreasing number of mere literary researchers. Only an irresponsible speculator can seriously suggest that the wisdom and learning embodied in books which have influenced mankind across the world and across the centuries – the Bible, the Koran, the Bhagavad Gita, *Das Kapital*, to say nothing of Confucius and Plato – can be communicated by electronic computers. James Thompson makes the point that the plays of Shakespeare were meant to be performed; but how can successive generations profit from the insights of the greatest Englishman if there are no texts available for proper study?

As new technology continues to lighten the burden of routine handling of books as physical objects, librarians must turn their attention towards the communication of contents. They must adopt a positive, matchmaking role, introducing readers to new authors, new thought, new insights. They must, as Cotton des Houssayes says, have an exact knowledge of all the arts and sciences, together with 'that exquisite politeness which attracts the affection of their visitors as their merit ensures their esteem'. This requires not the neglect of traditional skills but their enhancement; not the neglect of traditional media but their extension by means of the new. Libraries must not neglect their role as repositories of the wisdom of ages, but become also mediators and promotors of communication, with librarians as active participants in the process, their participation deriving from understanding of social needs and pressures, and from an informed consciousness of the importance of this activity. Librarians will contribute to the progress of humanity, not by disappearing in mass professional euthanasia, but through a positive professional creed which embraces with enthusiasm the prospect of a reading, as well as an informed, society.

In a paper to the 1979 Conference of the Scottish Library Association, I discussed the political and the literary contacts between Scots and English over the centuries. Although the political scene has been racked with discord, the literary tradition shows a deep and harmonious association which in my view has done far more to foster the concept of independent nationhood than any amount of physical combat. Dame Helen Gardner relates, in her preface to *The new Oxford book of English verse*, how she consciously doubted the propriety of including the Scots poets: 'But I decided that the Scots would be less offended at their inclusion under this title than at the omission of the Border Ballads and Burns, which are part of the cultural heritage of England as well as of Scotland'.

Science may be neutral, the same the world over, but national cultures are different and their literatures, their histories and traditions also differ, and make their own unique contribution to the universal cultural heritage of us all. In the developing countries, in countries whose people speak minority languages, it is a positive duty of librarians to encourage young authors, to foster and stimulate the use of the language to create a national literature and confident sense of nationhood. Such confidence will have no need of recourse to bombast and aggressive attitudes in the world community.

The future of mankind should not be towards greater uniformity, towards a set of standardized personalities in a Brave New World based on all receiving the same standard bits of information as if being programmed to act as machines. The future must be towards greater and richer diversity, encouraging each individual to develop his own unique personality based on unique experience enhanced by access to the thoughts of the greatest minds, enshrined in their books. Our concern must be for the quality of life no less than for the standard of living. What does it profit mankind to see three men walk on the Moon, when thousands are massacred in Assam through ignorance and lack of human understanding?

As Socrates found out, the search for wisdom, like the concept of nationhood, involves political activities. We should not shrink from this, because we can be sure that our abstention will not make it go away. I welcome the co-operation of the Library Association, Aslib, the Institute of Information Scientists, in discussing a National Information Policy, and I should wish these discussions to include members of other professions in the arena of Communication. Such a policy must take into account what people mean when they say 'Information', how it is presented, and the techniques and professional activities that society has developed to provide quick and accurate access to it. Such a policy ought also to take into account the reasons why people wish to communicate with each other, and the obstacles that some persons find it to their advantage to place in the way. Those who take cover in a pusillanimous retreat into the 'safe' areas of scientific and technical information delude themselves if they imagine that they are beyond the reach of politics.

All those engaged in Communication, whether as producers, intermediaries or consumers, would do well to consider and reflect on these questions, and particularly on the role they envisage for themselves in the society of the future. I do not doubt that none of them would seek to justify a divided nation, comprising an elite in control because they have access to information and time to make judgements about it, and a docile mass kept happy by a constant supply of trivia which require no mental effort because they contain nothing of human value.

The profession of librarianship and information science is itself a protest against such a division. To provide free access to information is a noble aim, provided that it embraces all kinds of information and does not decline into mere technical expertise. We have at our disposal already great stores of information to which access can be gained at the press of a button; we have small and cheap machines easy to operate in the comfort and seclusion of one's own home. We may look forward to better use of new technology, improved methods of information transfer from end to end of the global village, greater chances for the wretched of the earth to raise themselves to a decent standard of life.

All this has great value which I do not seek to denigrate. But it will be as sounding brass if not accompanied by greater understanding of the different manners and customs of other peoples, if instant information is followed by instant oblivion. For many people, the idea that technological progress leads to an age of cultured leisure is at present a hollow mockery; but a cultured society depends on the leisure to read, to consider and to make informed and sensible judgements, and such a society should be in prospect for all the people of this one world. A library must do more than facilitate access to bits of information; it should act positively in preserving human values which have, despite Man's inhumanity to Man, survived over the centuries. Librarians should take on the responsibilities of providing opportunity for intellectual and social development for the benefit of every individual in the human community, so that if and when the age of leisure does arrive, it will prove to have been worth the effort.

REFERENCES

Aitchison, Jean *and* Gilchrist, Alan
Thesaurus construction: a practical manual. Aslib, 1972.

Anderson, Dorothy
Universal Bibliographic Control. *International forum on information and documentation.* Vol 7, no 3, July 1982, pp10-14.

Barnes, Barry
T S Kuhn and social science. New York, Columbia UP, 1982.

Belkin, N J
Information concepts for information science. *Journal of documentation.* Vol 34, no 1, March, 1978, pp55-85.

Benge, Ronald
Communication and identity. Bingley, 1972.

Bertalanffy, Ludwig von
General System Theory. Allen Lane The Penguin Press, 1971.

Bertalanffy, Ludwig von
Robots, men and minds New York, George Braziller, 1967.

Beveridge, W I B
Seeds of discovery: a sequel to The Art of Scientific Investigation. Heinemann Educational Books, 1980.

Bramah, Ernest
The wallet of Kai Lung. Jonathan Cape, 1926.

Brandt, Willi, *Chairman*
North-South: a programme for survival. Report of the Independent Commission on International Development Issues. Pan Books, 1980.

Bronowski, Jacob
The Identity of Man. Heinemann, 1966.

Bruner, J S
The process of education. New York, Vintage Books, 1960.

Cornforth, Maurice
The open philosophy and the open society. Lawrence and Wishart, 1968.

Engels, Friedrich
Anti-Dühring. Lawrence and Wishart, 1934.

Foskett, A C
The subject approach to information. 4th edition. Bingley, 1982.

Foskett, D J
Classification for a general index language. Library Association, 1970.

Foskett, D J
Introduction to comparative librarianship. Bangalore, Sarada Ranganathan Endowment, 1979.

Glass, Bentley
The timely and the timeless: the interrelationships of science, education and society. New York, Basic Books, 1970.

Guilford, J P
Intelligence, creativity and their educational implications. San Diego, R R Knapp, 1966.

Gvishiani-Kosygina, Lyudmila A, *and* Vorotilin, Alexandr A
Universal Availability of Publications: the concept and programme. *International forum on information and documentation.* Vol 7, no 3, pp3-9.

Horton, Robin
  'African traditional thought and Western science'. In: *Knowledge and control.* Edited by Michael F D Young. London, Collier-Macmillan, 1971, pp208-266.

Hudson, Liam
  The cult of the fact. Cape, 1972.

Illich, Ivan D
  Tools for conviviality. London, Calder and Boyars, 1973.

International Telecommunications Union
  Guide to World Communications Year 83: development of communications infrastructures. (1982)

Irwin, Raymond
  The heritage of the English library. George Allen and Unwin, 1964.

Kemp, D A
  The nature of knowledge: an introduction for librarians. Bingley, 1976.

Kenyon, Sir Frederick
  Libraries and museums. Ernest Benn, 1930.

Koestler, Arthur *and* Smythies, J R, editors
  The Alpbach Symposium 1968. *Beyond reductionism: new perspectives in the life sciences.* Hutchinson, 1969.

Kuhn, T S
  The structure of scientific revolutions. 2nd edition. University of Chicago Press, 1974.

Lazlo, Erwin
  Introduction to systems philosophy: towards a new paradigm of contemporary thought. With a foreword by Ludwig von Bertalanffy. New York, Gordon and Breach, 1972.

Line, Maurice, *and* Vickers, Stephen
  IFLA's programme of UAP — Universal Availability of Publications. *International forum on information and documentation.* Vol 7, no 3, July 1982, pp8-9.

Luria, A R
  The making of mind. Edited by Michael Cole and Sheila Cole. Harvard UP, 1979.

MacBride, Sean, *Chairman*
  Many voices, one world. Paris, Unesco, 1980.

McGarry, K J
  Communication, knowledge and the librarian. Bingley, 1975.

Meadows, A J
  New information technology — integration or fragmentation of knowledge? *International forum on information and documentation.* Vol 7, no 4, October 1982, pp16-19.

Medawar, P B
  Pluto's Republic. OUP, 1982.

Medawar, P B
  Science and literature. *Encounter.* Vol 32, January 1969, pp15-23. The 1968 Romanes Lecture.

Mikhailov, A I *and* Giljarevskij, R S
  Guide for an introductory course on Informatics/Documentation, Paris, Unesco, 1970.

Mikhailov, A I *et al*
  Informatics — new name for the theory of scientific information. *Nanknotechnicheskaya informatsiya.* No 12, Moscow, 1966.

Piaget, Jean
  Structuralism. London, Routledge and Kegan Paul, 1969.

Polanyi, Michael
  Knowing and being. Routledge and Kegan Paul, 1969.

Popper, Karl R
Objective knowledge: an evolutionary approach. Oxford, Clarendon Press, 1972.

Ranganathan, S R
Prolegomena to library classification. 3rd edition. Bombay, Asia Publishing House, 1967.

Reid, L Arnaud
Ways of knowledge and experience. Allen and Unwin, 1961.

Thompson, James
The end of libraries. Bingley, 1982.

Unesco
World Conference on Cultural Policies, Mexico City, 26 July—6 August 1982. *Final Report.* Paris, 1982.

Unesco
World Congress on Books, London, 7—11 June 1982. *Final Report.* Paris, 1982.

Vickery, B C
'The nature of information science'. In: *Toward a theory of librarianship: Papers in honor of Jesse Hauk Shera.* Edited by Conrad H Rawski. Metuchen, New Jersey, The Scarecrow Press, 1973, pp146-168.

Vygotsky, L S
Thought and language. Edited and translated by Eugenia Haufmann and Gertrude Vakar. Cambridge, Mass, MIT Press, 1962.

Weiss, Paul A
The science of life: the living system — a system for living. New York, Futura Publishing Co, 1973.

Whitehead, A N
Science and the modern world. OUP, 1926.

Williams, Patrick *and* Pearce, Joan Thornton
The vital network: a theory of communication and society.
Westport, Connecticut, Greenwood Press, 1978.

Young, Michael, F D, editor
Knowledge and control: new directions for the sociology of education. Collier-Macmillan, 1971.

Ziman, John
Public knowledge: an essay concerning the social dimension of science. CUP, 1968.

INDEX

Abdus Salam 51
Academia Secretarum Naturae 22
Academy, Plato's 47
Adrian, *Lord* 73
Aitchison, Jean 98, 108
Alamogordo 3
al-Mustansir 22
al-Mustasim 22
Aldus Manutius 22
Alexander 21, 34, 49
American Psychological Association 35, 40
Anderson, Dorothy 56
Anglo-American Cataloguing Rules 29, 30
'Anomalous states' of knowledge 81, 93, 121
Archive science 19
Archives 58-9, 64, 68-9, 71, 75, 102, 122-
Archivists 114
Argentina 116
Aristotle 21-2, 31, 34, 49
Arnold, Matthew 48
Assam 127
Associated Press 118
Atomic Energy Authority 103
Authors, cataloguing 50

Bacon, Francis 23, 28, 49
Barnes, Barry 3
Beethoven, L van 42
Behaviourist psychology 70
Belkin, N J 35, 79, 81
Beveridge, W I B 53, 62
Bhagavad Gita 125
The Bible 125
Birmingham City Library 86
Bliss, H E 31, 98
Bodleian Library 18
Bohr, Niels 103
Book of Kells 49
Boswell, James 124
Boyle, Robert 23
Brandt, W 118
Brave new world 104, 113, 126
Brethren of Sincerity 22
British Association for the Advancement of Science 73
British humanities index 53
British Library 19, 32
British Library Lending Division 55, 57
British Library Reference Division 55-
British Museum 19, 29, 53, 55, 84

British Museum's General Catalogue of Printed Books 29
British national bibliography 52, 65, 95
British Standards Institution 30
Bronowski, Jacob 8, 42, 62, 69
Browsing 53
Bruner, Jerome S 89
Buffon, G 16

Carmina Burana 22
Casanova, Giacomo 47
Cataloguing 29, 50, 66, 82, 85, 90-
Caxton, W 22
Ceefax 98
Central Information Service, University of London 107
Chemical abstracts 25, 53-4, 65, 109
China 48
Citation Indexes 33, 63
City University 35
Clark, Kenneth 69
Classification 29, 30, 50, 66, 80, 85, 90-
Cleverdon, C W 81
Codes, cataloguing 50
Collection-building 19, 83
Concept formation 40, 89
Confucius 125
Cooke, Alistair 69
Cornforth, Maurice 120
Cotton des Houssayes, Jean B 107, 125
Cowley, Abraham 73
Cranfield 81
Creative scientist 60
Creative writer 51

Creativity 34, 42, 83
Crimean War 117
'Cultural imperialism' 118
Current awareness 88-
Cyrillic script 55

Darwin, Charles 62
Decimal classification 52, 92
Declaration of Independence 49
Declaration on Cultural Policies 10
Descartes, R 12, 15
Dewey, John, Society 39
Dewey, Melvil 30, 94
Dryden, John 23

Ecclesiasticus 8
The economist 24
Edison, Thomas A 15
Egyptians 21
Einstein, Albert 14, 103
Electronic mail 25
Engels, Frederick 37
Engineers Joint Council 108
ERIC Thesaurus 96
Euronet 83
Exchange Groups 26

Facet analysis 38, 97
Foskett, A C 79, 96
Free text indexing 95-

Galbraith, J K 86
Gardner, Helen 126
Garfield, Eugene 63
'Gatekeepers' 27
General Information Programme, Unesco 3, 33-4, 39, 59, 115
General Systems Theory 25, 31, 35

136

Giljarevsky, R S 77
Glass, Bentley 39
Goethe, J W von 47
'Golden chain' 47
Grandmother's footsteps 9
Gray, Thomas 43
'Grey' literature 29
Guilford, J P 40
Gutenberg, Johann 15, 109

Hamlet 4, 51
Hilton, A C 102
Hiroshima 3
Horton, Robin 9
'Housekeeping' 66
Hudson, Liam 40
Humpty Dumpty 2
Huxley, Aldous 70, 104
Huxley, T H 7

Illich, Ivan 1
Industry 20, 36, 72
'Informatics' 36, 77-
Information officers 2, 20, 76, 102, 123
Information science 2, 90
'Information service' 20, 88-, 103, 124
Information technology 64, 68, 102, 122-
Information Technology Year, 1982 1
Information theory 72, 81
Information transfer 64, 68, 75, 105, 113, 120-
Infrastructures 2
Institute for Scientific Information, Philadelphia 33, 63
'Intelibot' 122
'Intermediary' 109, 122
International Atomic Energy Authority 34

International Congress on UAP 57
International Council of Scientific Unions 33
International Council on Archives 34
International Federation for Documentation (FID) 30, 34
International Federation of Library Associations (IFLA) 34, 56, 114
International Programme for the Development of Communication 3, 34, 58, 72
International Standard Bibliographic Descriptions (ISBD) 56
International Standard Book Numbers (ISBN) 56, 66
International Standard Serial Numbers (ISSN) 56, 66
'The Invisibles' 23, 26
Irwin, Raymond 47

Johnson, Samuel 24, 124
Jonson, Ben 17
Jowett, Benjamin 89

Kai Lung 40
Kanazawa Industrial University 122
Kant, Immanuel 12, 15
Das Kapital 125
Kemp, D A 79
Kenyon, Frederick 53-4
Keywords 96, 98
The Koran 125
Kuhn, T S 3, 14, 61-
KWIC index 96

Latham, Robert 110
Leavis, F R 12

Leibnitz, G W 47
Library and Information
  Services Council 33, 35, 104
Library of Congress 19, 30,
  32, 54, 94-
Lindisfarne Gospels 49
Line, Maurice 57
Literature search 52, 93, 108
Lockheed Corporation 83
Lomonosov, M V 23
London Declaration 10
London, University of 65, 107
Loughborough University 35
LUCIS guide 107
Luria, A R 40
Lysenko, T D 124

MacBride Commission 116-
McGarry, Kevin 27, 79
McLuhan, Marshall 63
MARC Project 33, 95
Magna Carta 49
Manchester guardian 13
Manuscripts 59, 64
Mao Zedong 47
Market research 76-77
Medawar, Peter 12, 42, 60, 62
Mercury 13, 54
Microfiche 68
Mikhailov, A I 36, 76-
Mills, Jack 98
Milton, John 70
Molyneux, William 13
Moon exploration 71, 89, 127
Morris, William 10

1984 104, 113
NATIS 76, 115
National Academy of Sciences
  33
National Central Library
  54, 94

National Information Policy
  127
National Lending Library for
  Science and Technology 55,
  57
National libraries 72
National Science Foundation 33
Nature 5, 24
New Atlantis 28
New International Economic
  Order, Unesco 1
New World Information and
  Communication Order 1
News media 1, 18, 62, 69, 109
Newton, Isaac 12, 103
Nightingale, Florence 116
'Normal science' 63

Objective knowledge 120-
Orwell, George 104
Outreach 86

Panizzi, Antony 19, 84
Paperless society 10, 15, 63,
  68, 86, 104, 112, 123
Pasteur, Louis 41
Pearce, Joan 78
Pepys Library 110
Permuterm indexes 63
Pertinence 81-2, 86, 93
Philosophical transactions 24
Piaget, Jean 40-1
Plato 47, 125
Plutarch 21
Polanyi, Michael 119
Pope, J A 101-2
Popper, Karl 42, 119
Pragmatism 70
Precision 81
Prestel 98
Printing 15, 49
Privacy 67

Public libraries 19, 36, 67, 72, 85-6
Pushkin, Alexander 24
Putnam, Herbert 19

Radio 2, 15
The rambler 24
Ranganathan, S R 31, 38, 43, 65, 89, 97
Recall 81
Re-creation 45, 111
'Referees' 27, 113
Reference service 32, 45
Regional Library Bureaux 54
Relevance 43, 81-2, 86, 93
Renaissance 22, 48
Retrospective searching 88-
Reuter 118
Roget, Peter Mark 31, 97
Rote-learning 102
Royal Institution 17
Royal Society 23, 62
Royal Society of Arts 101
Russell, W H 116

Saunders, W L 104
Scott, C P 13
Selective Dissemination of Information 32, 98-
'Serendipity' 41, 83
Shakespeare, William 17, 42, 55-6, 86, 124-5
Skinner, B F 100
Sheffield University 35
Shera, J H 76
Sloane, Hans 13
Snow, C P 12
Socrates 12, 15, 127
Special library 36, 72, 85
The spectator 24
Spencer, Herbert 20

Sprat, Thomas 23
Subject catalogues 50, 95-
Sumerians 21
Systems analysis 25, 37
Systems Development Corporation 83

The tatler 24
Telecommunications 2
Television 2, 15
Thales of Miletos 21
Thesaurofacet 108
Thesaurus 96, 108
Thesaurus of engineering and scientific terms (TEST) 108
Third World countries 117-18
Thompson, James 125
Trade unions 67
Trevelyan, G M 117
'Two cultures' 12, 62

Unesco 1, 56, 76, 87
UNIDO 34
UNISIST 3, 33, 115
USSR 33
Universal Availability of Publications 57, 83, 114
Universal Bibliographic Control 56, 83, 114
Universal Context Fallacy 4
Universal Decimal Classification 30-1, 92
University Grants Committee 84
University library 36, 67, 72, 84
Urquhart, Donald 55, 57

VINITI 33, 36
Vickery, B C 90, 103
Video disc 110
Virtuosi 23

Vygotsky, L S 16, 40-1, 89

Wallace, A R 62
Waller, Edmund 23
Wandering Scholars 22
Watson, J D 63
Weekly memorials for the ingenious 24
Weiss, Paul 70, 100
Wheldon, Huw 54
Whitehead, A R 14
Williams, Patrick 78

Wordsworth, William 7
World Communications Year 1, 9
World Conference on Cultural Policies 10, 20, 47, 58, 60, 64, 114, 121
World Congress on Books 10, 57, 114, 121
Wren, Christopher 23
Writing, invention of 48

Ziman, John 3, 28, 36, 62, 80, 103

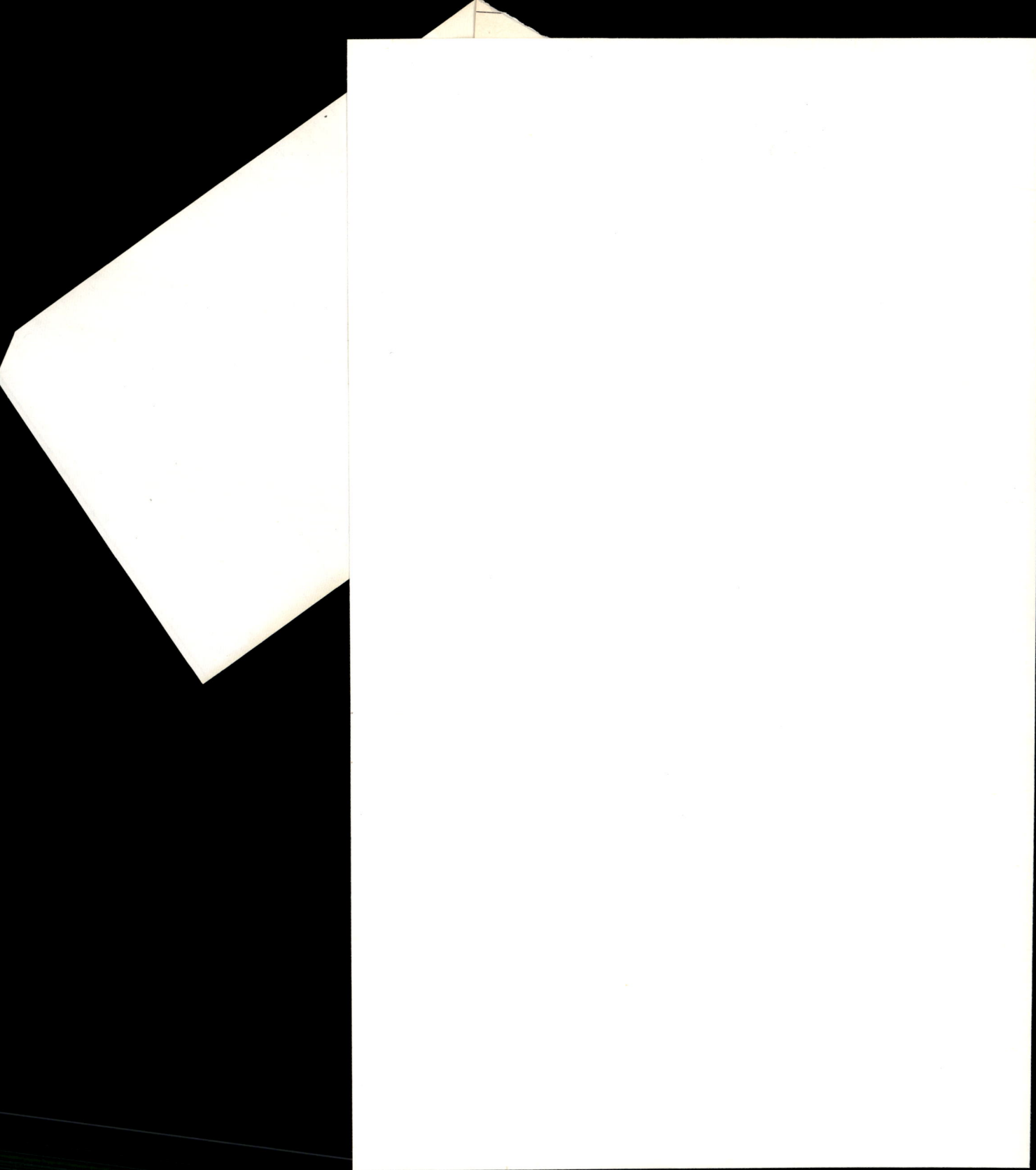

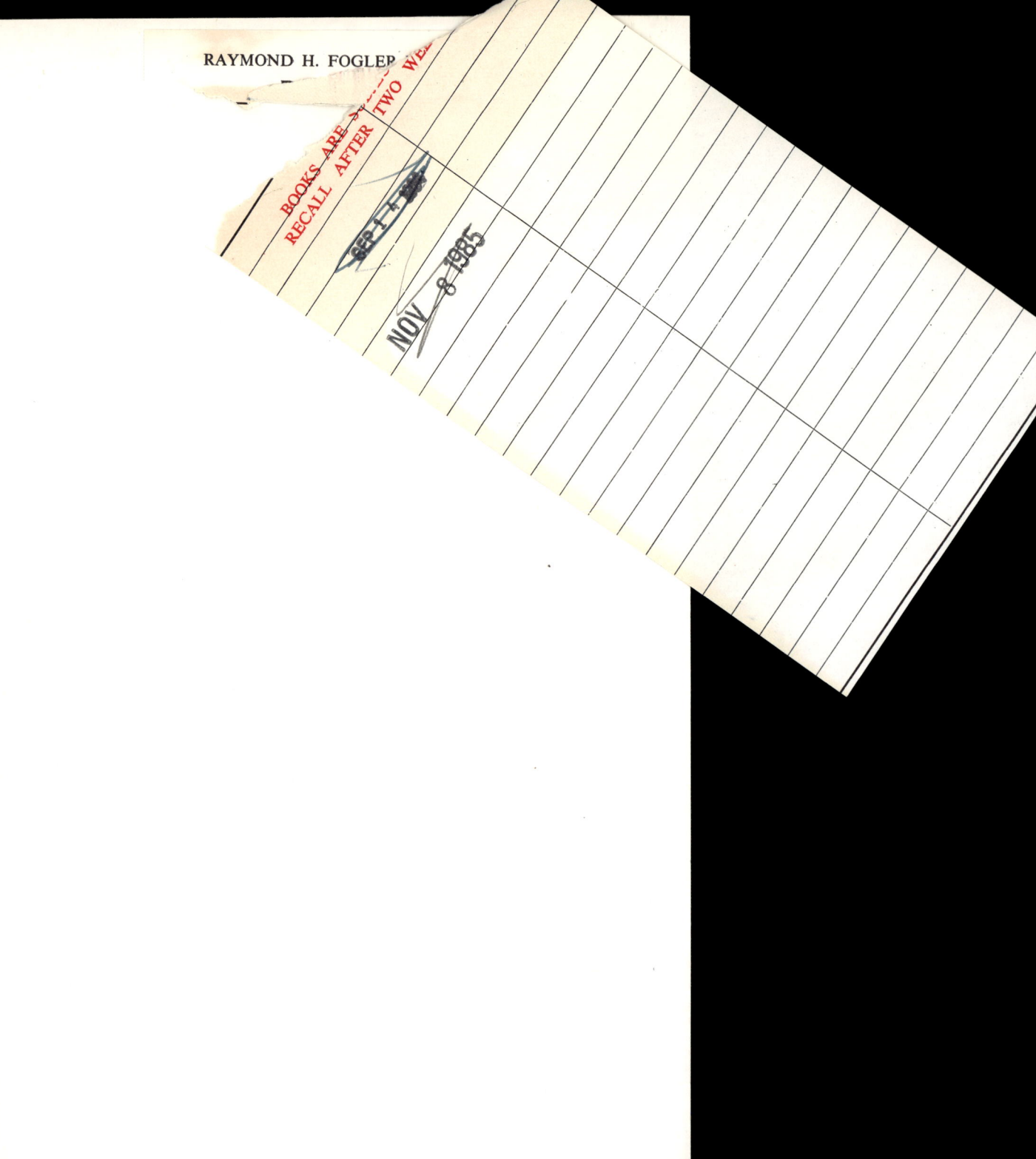